This book shows you how to release your subconscious brakes to inner peace and high performance. You learn how to stop worrying and start succeeding—immediately!

—Brian Tracy, author of *The Power of Charm*

Kase's understandable, clear guidelines for handling anxiety will change your life. She makes complicated paradoxes seem simple and teaches easy ways to manage them in your work days. Did you know that the way to overcome stress is the opposite from the way to overcome anxiety? You will find her short quizzes and exercises invaluable in helping you determine where you are with anxiety and what your next steps should be. This is one book you should NOT procrastinate in reading.

—Rita Emmett, author of *The Procrastinator's Handbook* and *The Clutter-Busting Handbook*

In today's competitive world, many people suffer from social anxiety and fear of failure in the workplace. With women entering the workforce at record rates, they are increasingly more prone to experience anxiety and worry in this arena. Luckily, Anxious 9 to 5 *provides a number of clear and simple solutions for each type of work-related anxiety problem. Full of wonderful real-life scenarios and examples, this book is certain to help many people who struggle with worries, fears, and doubts in the workplace.*

—Holly Hazlett-Stevens, Ph.D., assistant professor of clinical psychology at the University of Nevada, Reno, and author of *Women Who Worry Too Much*

If you want to make your life less complicated, less stress-ridden, and be able to maximize your full potential, then read this book.

—Bob Losyk, professional speaker and author of *Get a Grip! Overcoming Stress and Thriving in the Workplace*

Most people spend at least forty hours of their week at work. For people who have difficulties with anxiety, many more hours per week are spent worrying about work. There is no doubt that this kind of anxiety and worry interfere not only in work performance, but also in overall quality of life. Kase's book is a fantastic resource for anyone who is "anxious nine to five." The book is highly readable and includes a good dose of humor. Kase uses established cognitive behavioral techniques, best illustrated in the coaching points included in each chapter. These clear, concise activities help readers conceptualize their anxiety problems and effectively beat them. There is no doubt that readers who follow Kase's valuable advice will see an improvement in their work life and in their overall sense of well-being and happiness.

—Deborah Roth Ledley, Ph.D., associate director of the Adult Anxiety Clinic of Temple University and author of *Making Cognitive-Behavioral Therapy Work* and *Improving Outcomes and Preventing Relapse in Cognitive Behavioral Therapy*

Anyone with anxiety about his or her work who reads this book and applies Kase's coaching tips will be able to see fast results.

—Cindy Cashman, million-selling author and founder of www.cindycashman.com

HOW TO BEAT WORRY, STOP SECOND-GUESSING YOURSELF & WORK WITH CONFIDENCE

LARINA KASE, PSY.D., MBA

New Harbinger Publications, Inc.

Publisher's Note

This publication is designed to provide accurate and authoritative information in regard to the subject matter covered. It is sold with the understanding that the publisher is not engaged in rendering psychological, financial, legal, or other professional services. If expert assistance or counseling is needed, the services of a competent professional should be sought.

Distributed in Canada by Raincoast Books

New Harbinger Publications, Inc.
5674 Shattuck Avenue
Oakland, CA 94609

Cover and text design by Amy Shoup; Acquired by Catharine Sutker; Edited by Amy Johnson

---

Library of Congress Cataloging-in-Publication Data

Kase, Larina.
Anxious 9 to 5 : how to beat worry, stop second-guessing yourself, and work with confidence / Larina Kase.
p. cm.
ISBN-13: 978-1-57224-464-1
ISBN-10: 1-57224-464-X
1. Job stress. 2. Work—Psychological aspects. I. Title.
HF5548.85.K37 2006
158.7'2—dc22

2006017700

08 07 06
10 9 8 7 6 5 4 3 2 1
First printing

This book is dedicated to the clients who have allowed me to walk with them through their fears and worries into happiness, peace, courage, and success. You are a testament to the ideas in this book and proof that we can all overcome anxiety and create the careers we truly want.

Contents

Acknowledgments vii

Foreword ix

Introduction 1

CHAPTER 1
Your Hidden Problem 5

CHAPTER 2
Anxiety vs. Stress at Work 21

CHAPTER 3
When Perfectionism Is Problematic 39

CHAPTER 4
Your Own Worst Enemy 61

CHAPTER 5
When You Want to Stay Quiet 75

CHAPTER 6
The Fear of Failure That Leads to Failure 93

CHAPTER 7
The Behaviors You Think Help—But Don't 107

CHAPTER 8
Avoidance, Procrastination, and Anxiety 123

CHAPTER 9
The Nervousness That Flares Around Others 137

CHAPTER 10
You're in Charge—But You Don't Feel Like You Are 155

CHAPTER 11
The Workplace Worrier 173

CHAPTER 12

Your Confidence and Career Success **193**

Resources **203**

References **207**

Acknowledgments

I'd like to thank the mentors, supervisors, and educators who've taught me all I know about helping clients, especially the faculty and staff at the Center for the Treatment and Study of Anxiety at the University of Pennsylvania, and particularly my supervisors Edna B. Foa and David Riggs.

I greatly appreciate my colleague and friend Deborah Ledley for who she is as a person as well as for all of her helpful peer supervision. I value, too, Brian Ramirez and Eunice Kim, who are always only a phone call away. And I'm thankful for all of my incredible colleagues, including Martin Antony for his monumental contributions to the field, and Joe Vitale, who is the epitome of what you can achieve when you don't let anything hold you back.

This book greatly benefited from the thoughtful suggestions and editing of those at New Harbinger Publications, including Catharine Sutker and Amy Johnson. I've been moved by the dedication of the staff at New Harbinger to create books that will truly help people.

Thanks, too, to my parents, who taught me to relentlessly pursue knowledge and every one of my dreams (no matter how crazy they might seem!); to my sister, Nicole, who provides a wonderful example of living a successful, balanced life; to Moraima and John for believing in me without an ounce of doubt; to my uncle Roger for providing an example of a top businessperson, and to John, whom I appreciate beyond words.

Most importantly, I'd like to thank the coaching and therapy clients I've had the joy and privilege of helping. My clients are some of the brightest, most creative, and most inspiring people I've ever met. I learn from and appreciate them every day.

Foreword

What stops you from doing what you know has to be done eventually? What stops you from working with confidence and courage? In a recent movie I saw called *No Pain, No Gain*, a struggling bodybuilder looked in the mirror and said, "You're my nemesis."

It's the case every time. When you aren't taking action, when you're not happy, when you're avoiding speaking, working, or doing anything you know in your heart is the right thing to do, the only block is you. But how do you resolve that inner conflict so you can move forward with power, speed, and optimism? That's where this book comes in.

I've known Dr. Larina Kase for more than two years. We coauthored a book called *What's Stopping You? How to End Self-Sabotage for Aspiring E-Book Authors*. I've learned that any internal conflict can be cleared using her methods, and I'm delighted that she's finally sharing her workplace-oriented techniques with this book.

Read this gem and you'll discover how to overcome anxiety and perfectionism in your work, focus on success and courage, lead others with confidence, beat public speaking anxiety, truly enjoy your work, and much more.

If you're wondering if this book is for you, or if you're doubting that this book will work for you, then you need this book. Those worries and doubts are exactly what this book addresses.

Read this now.

Freedom awaits.

—Joe Vitale

Introduction

"Nothing is work unless you'd rather be doing something else."

—GEORGE HALAS
(FOUNDER AND LONGTIME
COACH OF THE CHICAGO BEARS)

We all know what it feels like to be anxious or frightened. Physically, anxiety is often associated with sensations such as a racing heartbeat, dizziness, breathlessness, sweating, muscle tension, headaches, abdominal discomfort, and general feelings of uneasiness. When we're anxious, we tend to focus on the situations and objects that trigger our anxiety; we tend to interpret situations more negatively. In our attempts to reduce our discomfort, we're driven to avoid feared situations, to distract ourselves from anxiety-provoking thoughts and images, and to protect ourselves from potential harm. In other words, anxiety is the feeling you get when you'd rather be doing something else. In the workplace, anxiety can make work feel like work. This book is all about dealing with anxiety at work.

In many cases, anxiety about work is a good thing. After all, it's probably your concern about potential negative consequences that gets you to work on time, motivates you to get your work done, and ensures that you do the best job you can. If you had no anxiety at all, you might not be as valuable an employee as someone who has at least some anxiety. Anxiety is only a problem if it occurs too frequently, too intensely, or in a way that interferes with your life. Chances are, if you're reading this book, you—or someone you care about—is experiencing work-related anxiety at a level that is a problem.

This book discusses a wide range of topics related to managing anxiety at work, focusing on three major anxiety culprits: perfectionism, social anxiety, and chronic worry. *Perfectionism* is the tendency to set standards or goals that are unrealistically high—and then to be negatively affected when your standards aren't met. Perfectionism can be associated with all sorts of problems, including nervousness around other people (due to a fear of making a less-than-perfect impression), obsessive-compulsive behaviors (for example, a tendency to be overly focused on irrelevant details, or a tendency to check one's work repeatedly), general worries (about job performance, getting things done on time, and other areas), depression, and anger. Perfectionism can be focused on oneself (for example, concerns about not meeting your own standards) or on others (such as excessive frustration when others don't meet your standards). It can lead people to spend too much time on tasks, to argue with coworkers, and to put off important projects for fear of not completing them perfectly.

Research suggests that about 80 percent of people experience *social anxiety* or shyness in certain situations or at certain times in their lives. People who are socially anxious are often shy, easily embarrassed, and overly concerned about what others think of them. For many people, these feelings of anxiety are manageable. However, about 30 million Americans experience social anxiety, shyness, and performance fears at a level that interferes with their lives—particularly their relationships, work life, and school. In the workplace, social anxiety can make it difficult or impossible for people to give presentations at work, socialize with coworkers, speak up in meetings, talk on the phone, communicate with clients or customers, talk to a boss or other authority figure, deal with conflict assertively, or even interview for a job in the first place!

Worry refers to the tendency to mull over anxiety-provoking thoughts—over and over again. Like social anxiety and perfectionism, worry isn't necessarily a problem. However, when your worries keep you awake at night or cause other difficulties such as poor concentration at work, muscle tension, or irritability, your worries may be getting the best of you. Work is often a focus of concern in people who worry too much. Worriers may worry about getting to work on time, doing a good job, making a good impression on their boss, or running out of money. Although perfectionism and social anxiety are often associated with worry, frequent and chronic worrying can also be about other aspects of work, aspects that aren't related to doing things perfectly or making a good impression on other people.

As problematic as worry, anxiety, and fear can be, there's every reason to believe that you'll be able to use the strategies described in this book to experience a significant improvement in your anxiety—or even overcome it completely. Dozens of clinical research centers around the world have studied these techniques and have found them effective in improving various types of anxiety-based problems.

This book will both help you understand the differences between stress and anxiety and help you develop a better understanding of how your own anxiety affects you in the workplace. In this book, you'll discover ways of dealing with perfectionism, fear of public speaking, fear of failure, anxiety about supervising others, and general worries that affect you at work. You'll learn to combat the tendency to engage in self-defeating patterns of thinking that contribute to anxiety. You'll discover ways to confront anxiety-provoking situations head-on, rather than avoiding them or relying on safety behaviors to feel more comfortable. The road to reducing anxiety may be bumpy, but if you stay the course, you'll get there.

Good luck!

—Martin M. Antony, Ph.D., ABPP
Director, Anxiety Treatment and Research Centre,
St. Joseph's Healthcare, Hamilton
Professor, Department of Psychiatry and Behavioural
Neurosciences, McMaster University

CHAPTER 1

Your Hidden Problem

"I'm not afraid of storms, for I'm learning how to sail my ship."

—LOUISA MAY ALCOTT

You're Not Alone

Millions of people experience anxiety. And although some of these individuals experience anxiety disorders—like panic disorder or social phobia—many do not have an anxiety disorder at all, but simply "normal" levels of anxiety.

As a psychologist, my area of specialty is anxiety disorders. As an executive coach, I've helped everyone from senior-level executives with jitters about deal-breaker meetings to managers uncomfortable interacting with colleagues to small business owners whose businesses suffer because they're always worried about getting everything done just right. All of these people are highly successful go-getters—who just happen to become anxious in particular workplace situations.

In this book, I'm going to walk you through the most common ways that anxiety rears its head in the workplace. Step by step, we'll go through both how to identify the signs of anxiety and how to overcome it. We'll start with a brief assessment to determine which particular types of workplace anxiety describe you. Then you can pick and choose which chapters to focus on—or read the book straight through. All chapters have how-to steps and coaching points (exercises) to help you manage and treat your anxiety.

We have a lot ahead of us: We'll start by identifying precisely how workplace anxiety comes up for you, and then go over the primary components of anxiety and how they interact with each other. Next, we'll clarify the differences between anxiety and stress and the different strategies the two require (chapter 2). We'll then focus on a very common anxiety culprit: perfectionism (chapter 3). After that, we'll explore self-defeating thought patterns (chapter 4), fears of speaking up and giving presentations at work (chapter 5), and the self-fulfilling aspects of our fears of failure (chapter 6). We'll then investigate behaviors that negatively impact anxiety: behaviors that seem likely to help but don't (chapter 7) as well as the vicious cycle of avoidance and anxiety (chapter 8). We'll examine anxiety in different types of social situations, looking first at discomfort in professional social and performance situations (chapter 9) and then at the anxiety involved in supervising and leading others (chapter 10). We'll then concentrate on worriers and worrying (chapter 11). And finally, we'll discuss how to use the ideas you've learned to help you create a highly successful career (chapter 12).

Are you ready to learn how anxiety from nine to five is holding you back from an enjoyable career and confidence at work? If so, grab a notebook and read on!

Anxious Nine to Five Self-Assessment

To help you pinpoint ways in which anxiety, fear, and worry about your job come up for you, I've created the following questionnaire. The questionnaire will quickly help you target the key areas in which anxiety, fear, and worry affect you. The scoring section will help you determine which areas are primary for you and which chapters address those particular areas. Focus on these sections of the book. I do, however, recommend reading the entire book—sections which may not immediately appear applicable to you may still contain material that can help.

The Questionnaire

Take the following brief questionnaire to see how anxiety comes up for you in the workplace. Please complete all items, rating how true each statement is for you personally, on a scale of 1–5. (Please choose a whole number for each item, not a fraction or a decimal.)

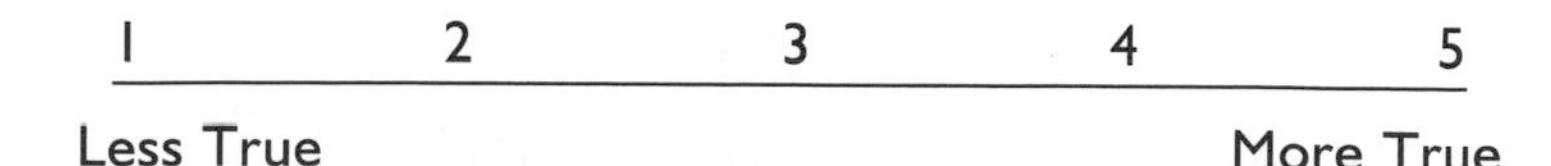

Less True More True

1. I find that my worrying about work isn't just related to the level of stress in my life—it may get worse with

stress, but the worrying sticks around regardless of my actual stress level. ______

2. In addition to stressful things like finances and a busy schedule, I feel nervous about some common aspects of work, like interactions with coworkers, my ability to do my job well, or how people at work view me. ______

3. Symptoms of anxiety that I sometimes experience at work include a racing heartbeat, trembling, shaking, sweating, worrying, feeling keyed up, difficulty in concentrating, being highly critical of myself, or anticipating the worst. ______

4. I usually don't feel satisfied with my work unless I feel it is done perfectly. ______

5. I have high, rigid standards for the quality of my work. ______

6. I sometimes fall behind on tasks because I spend so much time trying to do them just right. ______

7. I'm often highly critical of my work performance. ______

8. I frequently doubt my abilities to be very successful in my career. ______

9. In my job, I typically compare myself to others and find them much more impressive than I am. ______

10. When I need to give a presentation at work, I become highly nervous. ______

11. Speaking up in meetings is difficult for me. ______

12. I try to get out of giving oral reports and other presentations. ______

13. I typically expect the worst in my job. ______

14. I am very anxious about messing up at work. _____

15. I am more afraid of how my work will be evaluated than my coworkers and colleagues seem to be. _____

16. It's common for me to engage in behaviors to try to feel better at work, such as keeping my conversations short, planning out what I'm going to say, or mentally rehearsing conversations in my mind. _____

17. When I'm nervous about doing something at work, I'll often avoid that activity. _____

18. I frequently seek reassurance about my work performance. _____

19. Making professional contacts is intimidating to me. _____

20. I get anxious when interacting with my boss or other authority figures at work. _____

21. I frequently worry about how people will judge me in my job. _____

22. I've turned down—or failed to actively pursue—promotions due to fear. _____

23. As a boss, I feel like I am (or would be) a fraud—it all feels like an act or a front. _____

24. I become nervous when I have to give employees feedback or reviews. _____

25. I often worry about my job, even when I'm not there. _____

26. Sometimes I can't sleep because I am worrying about work. _____

27. I think I worry about my job and career more than other people do; this worrying interferes with my life or is distressing to me. _____

Scoring

Add up your answers in sets of three—first questions 1–3, then questions 4–6, and so on. Each three-question group targets a specific element of workplace anxiety. Any set of three with a total score of 8 or more is relevant to you, so for any set of questions in which you received a total score of 8 or more, read the relevant explanation below.

Questions 1–3: Anxiety and stress. If you scored 8–15 on this set of questions, you're likely to experience both workplace anxiety and workplace stress. A higher score within this range indicates a higher level of general anxiety about work. In chapter 2, Anxiety vs. Stress at Work, we'll discuss how stress and anxiety are different and how the ways to overcome them are actually the *opposite* of each other.

Questions 4–6: Perfectionism. If you scored 8–15 on this set of questions, you're likely to approach your work with perfectionism. While perfectionism can be beneficial at times, it's also often linked to anxiety. A higher score within this range indicates higher levels of perfectionism and anxiety. Read chapter 3, When Perfectionism Is Problematic, carefully and do all of the exercises.

Questions 7–9: Self-defeating thoughts. If you scored 8–15 on this set of questions, you probably experience self-defeating thoughts at work. You may be very critical of yourself and experience anxiety as a result. A higher score within this range indicates more significant self-sabotaging thinking. You'll learn how to change these thoughts in chapter 4, Your Own Worst Enemy.

Questions 10–12: Speaking anxiety. If you scored 8–15 on this set of questions, you're likely to be someone who becomes nervous about public speaking in a professional setting. This is a very common fear. In chapter 5, When You Want to Stay Quiet, we'll go over some of the keys to overcoming anxiety about speaking at work.

Questions 13–15: Fear of failure. If you scored 8–15 on this set of questions, you probably have a fear of failure regarding your work. A higher score within this range indicates greater worries about failure. Chapter 6, The Fear of Failure That Leads to Failure, identifies the common ways in which this fear comes up—and often results in your fear coming true.

Questions 16–18: Unhelpful behaviors. If you scored 8–15 on this set of questions, you probably engage in behaviors that you may think are helpful but actually aren't. In fact, many of these types of behaviors fuel anxiety. Because these behaviors are so important in causing and maintaining workplace nervousness, I've devoted two chapters to them: chapter 7, The Behaviors You Think Help—But Don't, and chapter 8, Avoidance, Procrastination, and Anxiety. Read both chapters carefully and do all of the exercises.

Questions 19–21: Interpersonal discomfort. If you scored 8–15 on this set of questions, you're likely to experience discomfort about interacting with coworkers. You may feel more uncomfortable in structured work situations or you may feel more uncomfortable in less structured, more social work situations. Either way, you'll learn some strategies for overcoming this discomfort in chapter 9, The Nervousness That Flares Around Others.

Questions 22–24: Being the boss. If you scored 8–15 on this set of questions, you're likely to either feel nervous about your role as a boss, or have intentionally avoided becoming a boss altogether. People with this form of apprehension often feel like they're not worthy to be in a supervisory role and worry about offending others and appearing self-centered. We'll address this form of anxiety in chapter 10, You're in Charge—But Don't Feel in Charge.

Questions 25–27: Worry about work. If you scored 8–15 on this set of questions, you're probably a workplace worrier. You're likely to be someone who both thinks a lot and whose thoughts often shift to fears and concerns. Read chapter 11, The Workplace Worrier, carefully and practice the recommended exercises to gain control over your worries.

How Anxiety Works

Now that you have a sense for how your nervousness comes up in the workplace, let's take a step back and explore what creates, increases, and maintains anxiety.

The Model of Anxiety

One of the most effective treatments for anxiety is cognitive behavioral therapy. Cognitive behavioral therapy has roots in both the research of Aaron Beck, "father of cognitive therapy," and the behavioral studies of dozens of psychiatrists and psychologists, beginning decades ago with Pavlov and Skinner. The cognitive behavioral framework provides a way to understand how anxiety works through the interaction of our thoughts, behaviors, and biological responses.

Thoughts

The thinking patterns that we engage in often begin or increase feelings of tension and uneasiness. In fact, it's almost impossible to become nervous without some form of anxiety-producing or anxiety-maintaining thought. You may not necessarily be aware of these thoughts, but that doesn't mean that they're not there at the heart of what's making you nervous.

Thinking can become distorted when we are distressed. Anxiety-based thoughts are often irrational or distorted. Below is a list of common anxiety-based thought processes. See if any of them sound like what happens to you. Also, next time you feel nervous, ask yourself if one of these types of thoughts went through your mind.

Magnification. This is when you overestimate how horrible something is likely to be. It's a catastrophic type of thinking process: consequences become worse with each chain of the thought. A thought that shows magnification is: "If I don't do a perfect job on this report, my boss will be disappointed and won't give me more important projects. I won't get promoted and won't get a raise. As a result, I won't be able to afford my mortgage. I'll end up getting laid off since my work is subpar—then I really won't be able to pay my mortgage and my house will be foreclosed upon."

All-or-none thinking. This is an extremely common form of thinking with anxiety. It's basically when you think that if a situation isn't great, it must be horrible. You see things in either black or white and aren't aware of the shades of gray in the middle. For example, "If I show any small signs of anxiety, people will think I'm an incompetent mess."

Fortune-telling. This is when you mentally predict the future, somehow knowing it will be disastrous in a big way. An example of this type of thinking is: "If I get up there and give a presentation, I'll flub it up and everyone will lose all respect for me and I'll never be promoted."

Minimization. This is usually exemplified by underestimating your ability to cope with the difficulties of a situation. We often mysteriously forget our own resourcefulness and ability to cope even in tough situations. We assume both that something bad will happen *and* that we won't be able to handle it. "If I forget to make that important point, there is no way I could ever recover."

Probability skewing. Often when people are nervous, they overestimate how likely it is that something negative will happen. This is because of something called *state-dependent memory*—we tend to remember and focus on those times in which we were in a mood similar to the mood we are in now. If you're about to face the CEO of your company and are feeling highly nervous, you'll remember other times you were nervous. If during just one of those times a negative consequence occurred, you'll assume the same outcome will occur again. An example of this type of distorted thinking is: "The chance of my making a huge mistake on this project feels 100 percent likely to occur."

Behaviors

One of the primary components of anxiety that interacts with thought patterns is behavior. The interaction between thoughts and behaviors is a chicken/egg type of relationship. Sometimes the first component of the cycle may not be obvious; other times it's very obvious.

Thoughts clearly influence behavior. You might have the thought, "If I go ask my boss for a raise, she may laugh at me and say that I don't deserve one." This thought could then influence your behavior—you may not ask for the raise as a result, or if you do, you may ask for it in a less confident manner. Or, for another example, you might worry about turning in a project that you've only proofread one time. If you're worried it has errors or is imperfect in other ways, these thoughts can then directly influence your behavior, compelling you to spend a lot of time reading through it and revising it.

At other times, anxiety-increasing thoughts can arise after behaviors or actions. For example, in a social situation with some of your coworkers, you might realize that you're beginning to blush. You may then think, "They can tell I'm nervous and will think less of me."

Clearly, in terms of anxiety, there is a strong relationship between thoughts and behaviors. Also, if you have an experience at work that you interpret as negative in some way, you'll be more likely to feel nervous in a similar situation in the future. As a result, you'll most likely try to avoid those types of situations or engage in specific behaviors to make them feel easier.

We'll delve deeper into specific behaviors that exacerbate anxiety in chapters 7 and 8. For now, begin to think about some things that you do that might feed into your anxiety at work.

Biology

One of the most obvious aspects of anxiety is physiological response. The following is a list of physiological responses that can occur with anxiety. Do any of them come up for you?

Physical Symptoms of Anxiety:

- Pounding or racing heart
- Sweating
- Trembling or shaking
- Lump in your throat or difficulty swallowing
- Blushing
- Feeling hot or cold
- Clammy hands
- Feeling dizzy or light-headed
- Increased rate of breathing
- Feeling unreal or out of it
- Breathlessness or difficulty catching your breath
- Feeling restless or jumpy
- Appearing pale or flushed
- Dry mouth

Why you feel like this. Anxiety is often created by worries about experiencing fear. While both anxiety and fear serve to protect us from danger (or perceived danger), in the moment that we experience them, they feel like they're actually hurting us.

When you experience sensations like those described in the list above, it's your sympathetic nervous system—your body's natural fight-or-flight system—kicking in. This is known as the *adrenaline response.* You feel afraid of something (public embarrassment, ridicule, a personal sense of failure, etc.) and your adrenaline kicks in, making you want to fight, flee, or freeze (do nothing).

The sympathetic nervous system naturally interacts with your interpretations of events and the behaviors you engage in. Fortunately, we're hardwired to habituate to this: our fearful physiological responses naturally decrease over time. This reduction in anxiety occurs as a result of our parasympathetic nervous system's response. Think about it—have you ever stayed at a heightened level of anxiety for multiple hours or days? Because your body naturally habituates, it's actually impossible to remain at your peak level of anxiety for a very long time.

Throughout this book, I'll provide you with strategies to make your physical responses to anxiety-provoking work situations work for you rather than against you.

Why Anxiety Works at Work

It's common to feel nervous about things related to work because, let's face it, work is a big deal. We all have a lot riding on our careers. We may have spent years of education getting ready for our job or invested years in working our way up. We need to support ourselves and our families with the income from our jobs and we have a human need to do well and be recognized for our achievements.

Anxiety is like a mosquito trying to get into a room filled with tasty people—it will try to get in wherever it can. The mosquito bite is a good analogy for anxiety: while it's definitely uncomfortable, it's not actually dangerous (assuming for the purpose of my example that the mosquito doesn't have West Nile or some other awful virus and that you're not allergic), and it's temporary. And while the itching and swelling of a bite will go away over time if you leave it alone, the more you scratch it the worse it will become. The same is true for anxiety: It's not dangerous, and it will go away if you respond the right way.

Imagine This . . .

Wouldn't your work life be nice if you weren't nervous, uneasy, on edge, apprehensive, or uncomfortable? Try to picture how your life would look and be different without the companion of workplace anxiety.

It may be hard to imagine what this would even be like. However, creating a vision for how you'd like to become is an essential first step in making change. A Japanese proverb makes this point dramatically: "Vision without action is a daydream. Action without vision is a nightmare." Or, as Yogi Berra more simply put it, "If you don't know where you're going, you may wind up somewhere else." Before you can start taking action toward change, you need to know where you're trying to go.

On Your Way . . .

Now that you know how workplace anxiety functions, we'll begin working on how to beat it. In the next chapter you'll discover how anxiety and stress are commonly misunderstood and confused. This is extremely important because the way to handle anxiety is actually the opposite of the way to handle stress. Sound strange? Read on!

coaching points

1. **Picture How It Looks**

   Ask yourself: how would work and home life look without anxiety? Take a moment and really try to picture what this would look like for you.

   Maybe you'd get out of work earlier because you wouldn't be obsessing about a memo or project. Or maybe you'd enjoy nights of restful sleep, with no interruptions from work-related worries. Or maybe you'd easily and fearlessly give presentations. Or maybe you'd chat comfortably with colleagues at the watercooler.

   Think about how you would seem different in a worry-free work situation, both to yourself and others. What would other people notice as being different?

   Take out your notebook and write down several sentences to describe what specifically would look different, including what would be removed (e.g., stuttering speech) and what would be added (e.g., confident projection of voice).

2. **Think About How It Feels**

   To make this vision of change even more palpable and compelling, picture how you'd actually feel in the situation. Select the words from the following list that best describe the new feelings that you would experience without work-related anxiety in your life. Pick the five that are most important to you.

   - Confident

coaching points

(continued)

- Free
- In control
- In charge
- Physically calm
- Relaxed
- Content
- Energized
- Competent
- Like a strong leader
- Likeable
- Attractive
- Intelligent
- Peaceful
- Like a valuable team member
- Secure
- Worry-free

3. **Consider How Your Work Performance Changes**

The last step in creating a strong vision of how your career will be once it's no longer hampered by anxiety is to look at its impact on your work performance. Because workplace nervousness typically impacts work performance, it's important to think about what would change and what would stay the same. In your notebook, brainstorm the impact that overcoming your anxiety at work will have on your work performance. Will you be more efficient in your work? Will you feel more calm and appear more poised? Will you take risks and pursue new opportunities?

coaching points

(continued)

As you're doing this exercise, you may find that you're reluctant to let go of some of your anxiety-producing habits. For example, people often fear that if they let go of their perfectionism, the quality of their work could suffer. Alternatively, you might worry about the increased expectations and responsibilities that you'd have to deal with if your work performance improved. Write down any fears or concerns you have about overcoming your anxiety at work.

Recognize, too, that these changes may affect your work both positively and negatively. Actually, you may find that the negative impact of these changes is balanced by positive changes in other areas of your life. When one executive client I worked with overcame her nervousness about speaking in meetings, she actually decided to remain in her current position rather than move to a higher one. She recognized that many of her efforts to be promoted arose from a feeling that she needed to prove herself. When she was no longer uncomfortable with herself, she realized that other areas of her life (exercise, family, fun, etc.) were at least equally important to her as her work and were things she didn't want to sacrifice by accepting a promotion.

CHAPTER 2

Anxiety vs. Stress at Work

> Stress is an orphan that has no home, unless and until you adopt it.
>
> —ROBERT XAVIER HOGAN

Are You Anxious? Or Are You Stressed?

Do you know whether you're anxious or stressed at work? If you're like most people, you probably don't. You probably think they're the same thing. They're actually quite different.

The difference between anxiety and stress is critical. Unfortunately there's a commonly held misconception that they're the same thing—or at least very similar things. I used to believe this myself and would use the terms interchangeably. In fact, I didn't learn the fine nuances between them until I worked at the Center for the Treatment and Study of Anxiety at the University of Pennsylvania.

The reason that you need to understand the difference between anxiety and stress at work is simple: *the way to overcome anxiety is actually the opposite of the way to overcome stress.*

In this chapter, I'll explain how to distinguish between anxiety and stress and begin to show you how to overcome both. Once you understand the differences, you'll be able to more effectively tackle the difficulties you experience at work.

The Relationship Between Anxiety and Stress

You've probably heard a lot about stress in the workplace. Stress at work is very common and is typically the cause of *workplace burnout.* Workplace burnout involves feeling overwhelmed, overtaxed, understimulated, undervalued, and fatigued with your job.

There are many books on the topic of stress at work but few on anxiety at work (hence the need for this book!). Here are some of the similarities and key differences between anxiety and stress in regard to thought patterns, physiological responses, and behaviors.

Thought Patterns with Anxiety and Stress

Thought processes differ slightly in anxiety and stress. In general, anxiety is associated with being nervous or afraid, while stress is linked with feeling overwhelmed or taxed. Of course, there's a good deal of overlap here—stress can sometimes trigger anxious thinking. Similarly, anxiety can tax your ability to cope with stress, making your stress that much worse.

Anxious Thoughts

Anxious thoughts are characterized by words like:

- Afraid
- Nervous
- Frightened
- Apprehensive
- Uncomfortable
- Fearful
- Worried
- Edgy
- Jumpy
- Uneasy
- Panicky
- Tense
- Alarmed
- Unnerved
- Scared
- Doomed
- Disastrous
- Embarrassed
- Intimidated
- Unsettled
- Upset
- Fidgety
- Restless

Stressed-Out Thoughts

Some words that are more specific to stressful thoughts include:

- Taxing
- Demanding
- Overwhelming
- Strenuous
- Wearing
- Tiring
- Exhausting
- Draining
- Grueling
- Arduous
- Fatiguing
- Tiresome

Thoughts Common to Both Anxiety and Stress

As I've mentioned, there is some overlap between the thinking patterns characteristic of stress and anxiety. Here are some of the words that come up with both:

- Tense
- Upset
- Uncomfortable
- Sleepless
- Unsettled
- Worried

Physical Responses with Anxiety and Stress

A clear pattern emerges from the lists of words above. With anxiety, your thoughts race and jump around toward the worst-case scenario; with stress your thoughts are likely to feel hazy or out of focus (it can feel like there are so many things to remember that it's impossible to focus on any single one).

Anxiety entails being physiologically revved up or on edge. Stress, on the other hand, involves being fatigued and exhausted. A useful analogy is that of a spring: anxiety feels like you're a spring wound very tightly. There's a great deal of tension. You may feel like you could snap at any point in time. Anxiety may also feel like a spring being opened and closed quickly. For this reason, anxiety makes you feel tense, wound up, drained, and on edge.

Stress, on the other hand, feels like a tensionless spring pinned down by a paperweight. Stress feels like a heavy weight on your back. You feel drained, but in a different way. Anxiety feels like you've just spent a lot of energy—stress feels like you just can't get together the energy in the first place. This is why you feel sluggish and fatigued when you're stressed. Let's look at the differences in how anxiety and stress feel in a little more detail.

How You Feel When You're Anxious

In chapter 1, we went through some of the ways that anxiety makes you feel. Anxiety usually produces physical symptoms like a racing heart, breathlessness, sweating, shaking, and dry mouth. These are the effects of your sympathetic nervous system getting you ready to fight, flee, or freeze.

Sometimes anxiety is characterized mainly by worry and apprehension (as opposed to panicky feelings). When this is the case, physical symptoms appear more similar to stress. These symptoms include tension, headaches and other muscle aches, restlessness, and an inability to relax.

How You Feel When You're Stressed

In general, the physical symptoms of stress include muscle tension, cramping, headaches, backaches, upset stomachs, eye strain, fatigue, and shallow breathing. With stress, it's unusual to see the adrenaline-rush symptoms you commonly see with anxiety. The physical signs of stress are, however, more similar to the physical signs of the worrying type of anxiety. This makes sense: worrying is associated with both anxiety and stress.

Behaviors Seen with Anxiety and Stress

Again, there's often overlap in the behaviors seen with anxiety and stress, particularly when you experience both. Since they commonly co-occur, you may recognize both types of behaviors; read through the following examples to see which behaviors are linked to anxiety and which are linked to stress.

Anxiety-Fueled Behaviors

There are two main forms of anxiety-fueled behaviors: *overcompensating behaviors* and *avoidance behaviors.* Overcompensating behaviors are the things you do to try to help yourself reduce your anxiety or make it less noticeable to others. These might include speaking quickly before you have time to say something dumb or spending extra time planning an event so you're sure you get everything right. You'll learn more about this interesting reaction to anxiety in chapter 7.

Avoidance behaviors include escaping from an anxiety-provoking situation early or avoiding it altogether. For example, you might avoid going to your office holiday party or attending a meeting when you need to give a presentation. You might also try to avoid the feeling of anxiety that comes up when you need to complete a project in a way that doesn't feel perfect—by trying to complete it perfectly.

The most common form of avoidance is procrastination. If you're a procrastinator, you probably know it! You may procrastinate by going to get a snack, checking your e-mail, talking to a friend, working on easier projects (that aren't due until after the project you really need to be working on), or complaining about how much work you have to do and how tight your deadlines are. We'll discuss avoidance behaviors in detail in chapter 8.

Stress-Driven Behaviors

Stress-driven behaviors typically involve trying to do too much. Since stress usually occurs when people are overwhelmed and overworked, people often respond by trying to get as many things done as they can, as quickly as possible. A common way to do this is multitasking. However, if you've ever tried to multitask at a time when you're feeling particularly stressed out, you know that it's not always very effective. You may miss important things, make mistakes, feel completely flustered and out of control, and end up taking even longer to finish whatever you're working on.

Avoidance is common to both anxiety and stress. A form of avoidance that occurs in response to stress is to shut down and not attempt to tackle anything. For example, let's say your pile of bills and paperwork has grown so tall that it stresses you out to even walk by it. Instead, you walk the other way and don't even think about dealing with it. This avoidance behavior differs from procrastination because procrastination means telling yourself that you *will* deal with it—just later.

Example Scenarios

To better illustrate the difference between anxiety and stress, let's go through a couple of examples. With each one, think about what does and doesn't sound like you.

Anxiety at Work

You feel afraid, intimidated, unsettled, and embarrassed when you're singled out in a meeting at work to describe a work process. You think that you didn't work enough on the project and that you can't answer questions about it in detail. After you hear your boss call your name, your pulse quickens and you feel short of breath. "Oh no!" you think, "I can't think of anything to say!" Your fear has been triggered—you want to slide under your seat and hide!

You wish you hadn't come to the meeting and try to think of an excuse to not respond. You manage to say something and you survive the meeting, but the rest of the day and much of the night is spent worrying about what you said and how people responded. "My boss looked disappointed in me. I wonder what he was thinking. He's probably already thinking of who to replace me with."

Your worrying keeps you up at night and you don't want to go to a meeting with your boss the next day.

Stress at Work

You walk into work on Monday morning and face a desk piled high with paperwork. "Ugh," you think to yourself, "I'll never be caught up." Before you can even turn on your computer, your phone rings and a coworker comes over and starts asking you questions. You'd like to help your coworker out, but know that you could get behind with your work for the day if you don't get started right away. You answer him with a quick response and say you'll try to catch up later in the day. Your week has only been ten minutes long and you're already overwhelmed!

You then find out that a project you'd thought was completed on Friday wasn't actually finished. It needs to go back on your already long to-do list. When you get around to checking your e-mail, you find several urgent requests by your boss. You think to yourself, "How am I ever going to hang in there until Friday?"

The Workaholic

A common phenomenon for both anxiety and stress in the workplace is workaholism. You probably know a workaholic—or perhaps you struggle with it yourself. Like any of the "isms," workaholism has a range of severity levels. One extreme includes the person who is so invested in working that she works every evening and weekend. Workaholics seem to live to work. Workaholism can easily ravage your personal life since the people in your life will feel that you have no time for them. Ironically, although the point of workaholism is to excel in your work, it can actually hold you back from being a top performer because of the stress, anxiety, and poor time management it leads to.

On the other end of the spectrum is the person who merely works to live: he goes to work because he needs to, but gets out of work as soon as possible. Somewhere in the middle is the person who is dedicated to her job, but also dedicated to other aspects of her life. I'd like to help you be in this middle zone, so that you both excel in your work and enjoy your life.

Anxious Workaholics

Anxiety and stress—or a combination of the two—can both lead to workaholism. First let's examine how anxiety leads to workaholism.

How Worry and Workaholism Are Connected

One primary component of anxiety is worry. If you're prone to worrying, you'll easily be able to imagine dozens of problems that could occur if you stopped working so much.

You may fear that if you didn't work so much, you'd lose your job, not earn enough money, have to deal with having a boring social life or difficult family situation, not do your work perfectly, face embarrassment in front of coworkers, or not get promoted. A logical response to these worries about horrible consequences seems to be to work harder and work more. This is how worry leads to workaholism.

Perfectionism Slows You Down

Another way that anxiety can cause workaholism is through perfectionism. This makes intuitive sense. When people are perfectionists, they feel that things are never good enough. The resulting behavior is to work and work until your work is as close to perfect as possible. If you work until everything feels completed just right, you'll clearly be working a lot. It's an unachievable dream: as a perfectionist, you'll probably still not feel that all of your hard work is good enough, making you want to work still harder and more. As you may know, working harder or more doesn't necessarily mean working smarter or better. We'll delve into perfectionism in greater detail in chapter 3.

Stressed Workaholics

Stress is both a cause and a result of workaholism.

Stress Causes Workaholism

When you feel highly stressed, you may be more likely to increase the amount you work. For example, if the cause of your stress is financial pressure, you may decide that the only way to alleviate your financial difficulties is to get a promotion. As a result, you may become highly focused on your work in an attempt to secure that promotion.

This type of workaholism may begin as situational or targeted to a specific stressor, but it can become an unhealthy habit if you repeatedly respond to stress by throwing yourself into your work at the expense of other areas of your life.

Stress Is Caused by Workaholism

As you may already know, stress often results from workaholism. Difficulty in delegating tasks to others can lead to feeling overwhelmed by work tasks. You may find yourself bringing work home with you and periodically working through evenings and weekends. This can be frustrating for members of your family; family pressure and stress can result. You may also end up neglecting your physical health and well-being because you work so much.

How to Deal with Anxiety and Stress

You may be wondering why I'm going to such lengths to help you understand the difference between anxiety and stress. Again, the reason is this: *the way to overcome anxiety is the opposite of the way to overcome stress*. This may sound strange—while anxiety

coaching point

Are you a workaholic? Be honest. If you have some workaholic tendencies, try the following exercise. Answer the following four questions to learn more about your workaholism and see whether it stems from anxiety, stress, or both.

1. What makes you work so much?
2. What are you afraid would happen if you worked less?
3. How does anxiety (including worrying or perfectionism) slow you down at work?
4. What stress in your life leads you to work more? How does working more create more stress for you?

and stress are clearly different concepts, they do share certain similarities. Let's look at specific ways of addressing anxiety and stress to help clarify why the strategies are different. We'll start with stress.

Try to Reduce Stress

You probably already know that the best way to manage stress is to get rid of it. If you're doing too much, figure out how to get some of your activities off your plate. If you have an annoying coworker who is making your life miserable, assert yourself to make the interactions lessen or change. (See chapter 10 for more about assertiveness.) If you have financial stress, work to increase your income or decrease expenses. There's no benefit to allowing stress to pile up and weigh you down.

Problem Solve

Problem solving entails looking for active methods to change the stressful situations; it's an effective strategy for managing stress. You might search for ways that people in your office could provide you with more support, or brainstorm ways to improve systems and work processes to make them more effective and efficient.

Another problem-solving strategy is to examine your role in the problematic situation. You may need to request training to gain new skills to help you do your job better. Or maybe you'd benefit from working with a communications coach to help you better interact with coworkers and present your ideas in an assertive (but not aggressive) manner. Or perhaps you could help yourself by analyzing your level of focus and considering how you become distracted from tasks—and thus increase both your stress and the time it takes to complete work projects.

Jim's Story: Distractions and Stress

Jim hired me to help him become more efficient at work. He wasn't anxious about his work, but he was experiencing stress due to the many hours he was working and pressure from his boss to produce improved output. We discovered that Jim was easily distracted by several specific things during his day, including e-mail, phone calls, and coworkers with questions. As a result, he wasn't able to focus and always felt overwhelmed.

To solve this problem, we structured his day more clearly. He scheduled times to check e-mail and voice mail and times to be available to colleagues. At all other times, he didn't check e-mail, didn't answer the phone, and didn't talk to colleagues. Although he had to struggle to resist the urge to pick up the phone or read his e-mail, when he changed his habits, his efficiency greatly went up and his stress went down.

Relaxation

Another important strategy for dealing with stress is to create more opportunities for relaxation and enjoyable activities to help you cope better. Many people become stressed because they don't engage in enough behaviors to refuel and regenerate themselves. If the majority of what you do is work or things that you need to do, then inevitably you're going to become stressed.

The types of relaxation activities that help you beat stress depend on your interests and personality. For some people, fast-paced, high-energy sports are invigorating and relaxing, while for others the best way to relax is to sit down in front of a favorite movie. The right relaxation activities can also depend on circumstances. For example, if you're a new parent and feel like you're constantly running around and on alert, the most relaxing thing for you may be a twenty-minute massage.

So, if the way to handle stress is to reduce it with problem-solving and relaxation activities, what about anxiety? Read on!

Try to Experience Anxiety

I've already given away the secret to dealing with anxiety: it's the opposite of how to deal with stress. So, if you're supposed to reduce stress, does that mean you are supposed to *increase* anxiety? Yes! I know it sounds completely crazy, but it's true. Ultimately, to truly overcome anxiety, you need to experience it at its highest level.

Bring It On

When you run from anxiety, it chases you—faster. When, on the other hand, you stand up and confront it, it eventually backs down. Anxiety is like the school yard bully that forces another kid to give him his lunch money. If you give the bully your lunch money every day, he's likely to keep bullying you. If, on the other hand, you stop giving him your money, he'll eventually realize that you aren't someone to pick on. Like the bully, anxiety may initially get worse when you stop backing down, but it will eventually subside. Anxiety likes the reaction it gets from you. When you stop reacting, it stops going after you.

You probably know that it is important to face your fears. When you avoid facing what makes you uncomfortable, your discomfort grows bigger and bigger and becomes more and more difficult to deal with. The strategy to overcoming anxiety is to purposefully allow yourself to experience it. This is distinctly different from dealing with stress. To reduce stress you don't need to face your biggest stress in the same way that you need to face your biggest fear to overcome your anxiety.

Let's say you're nervous about giving negative feedback to one of your direct subordinates. The employee is volatile and likely to get angry. You detest confrontation and anger—especially when it's directed at you. The feedback session looms in your mind, making you worried and anxious. What would happen if you put the session off for a week or two? Are you likely to feel better? Probably not. Most likely you'll grow increasingly uncomfortable about it, so that by the time you actually need to do it, it will feel like a very big deal indeed. If, on the other hand, you met with the employee right away and got it over with, it wouldn't be as big a deal, you wouldn't get as nervous, and you'd feel great for having done it—and probably have more confidence that you could handle similar situations in the future.

Stay With It

Another important component of managing anxiety is staying with it. It's not enough to just face it, you must face it long enough that you begin to feel better. All living creatures naturally habituate to anxiety if they stay in a situation long enough. Research has found that treatments for anxiety based on this principle of prolonged exposure can be very successful (Foa and Kozak

1986)—i.e., in order to habituate yourself to your fear, you need to expose yourself to a feared situation for a long period of time.

I recently witnessed a simple habituation to fear while training my puppy Maggie. Maggie was raised in the countryside and as a result, hadn't spent much time around cars. When she came to live with me in the city, she became frightened whenever she saw or heard a car. One day we sat down on the sidewalk and watched cars go by for forty-five minutes—not the most exciting forty-five minutes I've ever spent, but I didn't want my puppy to remain scared. At the end, she was significantly less frightened of cars.

Jen's Story: Habituating to Public Speaking

Jen always felt a rush of anxiety when she spoke up in meetings. When I asked her how she handled this anxiety, Jen told me that usually she'd just say something very brief and then try to relax. I explained to her that she was escaping from her anxiety too early and not allowing herself to habituate. I suggested that next time she try to speak twice as long. She, of course, did not like this suggestion, but she decided to try the idea out anyway. By the end of her longer statements, she did indeed feel a lot less nervous.

Do It Again

It's not enough to confront a situation once and expect to never feel anxious in the situation again. You'll need to do it several times. As a general rule, the more intense your anxiety, the more times you'll need to confront the anxiety-provoking situation.

In the case study above, Jen's anxiety about speaking up in important meetings was pretty intense, so she needed to speak up many times before she began to feel completely calm. As she spoke for slightly longer amounts of time, she was able to experience a reduction in her nervousness *while* she was speaking. And as she spoke in meeting after meeting, she also experienced a reduction in anxiety *between* meetings.

Anxiety Action Steps vs. Stress Action Steps

Throughout the rest of the book we'll be delving into how to overcome anxiety in detail. You'll see how strategies build on this idea of exposing yourself to your fears and you'll learn not only how you can handle them, but also how to use them to excel in your career. For now, my goal is for you to understand how anxiety and stress work, how they're different, and how the methods for overcoming them are opposite.

Another Paradoxical Idea

The concept of increasing your anxiety in order to get over it is paradoxical and counterintuitive. It's natural to want to avoid anxiety, escape from anxiety, or reduce anxiety. In the next chapter, we'll move into another paradoxical concept: perfectionism. Most people think that perfectionism is a good thing: it makes you perfect. Now, let's explore why this isn't necessarily true.

coaching point

In your notebook, do the following exercise over the course of the next two weeks:

1. Record all of the times you begin to feel uncomfortable or distressed regarding something to do with your work. These can be situations when you are at work or situations in which you're thinking about work or situations with coworkers outside of the office.
2. Create a column for anxiety and a column for stress. In each column, identify whether what you experienced was anxiety or stress or both.
3. In the appropriate anxiety or stress column, identify two or three specific strategies for overcoming the stress or anxiety. For stress, include specific examples of stress-reduction, problem-solving, and relaxation techniques. For anxiety, include specific ways to confront the anxiety, in a prolonged manner and multiple times.

CHAPTER 3

When Perfectionism Is Problematic

"I think perfectionism is based on the obsessive belief that if you run carefully enough, hitting each stepping-stone just right, you won't have to die. The truth is that you will die anyway and that a lot of people who aren't even looking at their feet are going to do a whole lot better than you, and have a lot more fun while they're doing it."

—ANNE LAMOTT

Are You a Perfectionist?

It's one thing to admit that you're a perfectionist and another to realize how your perfectionism is problematic. I had a client who swore that her tendencies to make everything just right were helpful. She did eventually become a recovering perfectionist but first had to overcome some key beliefs. Here's her story—does any of it sound like you?

Rosanna's Story: Recognizing Perfectionism as a Weakness

Rosanna always knew that she was a perfectionist. In fact, she greatly valued this quality in herself. Others made it clear that they did, too. Teachers and professors told her she was one of the most dedicated students they'd ever had, and her parents often boasted to others about what a high achiever she was.

When Rosanna was a student, she would become upset if she received a 90 on a test; she'd labor over papers to make sure that she got the wording just right. These tendencies stuck with her as she embarked on her career in marketing.

Although Rosanna created some of the highest quality reports for her company, she also frequently got behind in her work and frustrated her coworkers. Through the process of coaching, Rosanna learned that her perfectionism was actually both her biggest strength and her biggest weakness. Rosanna told me, "It's funny how what helps you also hurts you."

While it was difficult for Rosanna to give up some of her perfectionism, when she finally did, she found that she was able to finish her work more quickly and—much to her surprise—that the quality of her work was even better.

Perfectionism Quiz

(Be Sure to Get 100 Percent—Just Kidding!)

Many people who are perfectionists realize it. Others do not. Alternatively, you might be aware of your perfectionism in some aspects but not others. Complete the following short quiz to learn how strong your work-related perfectionism is. Judge each statement on a scale of 1–5 with 1 = not at all true, 2 = sometimes true, 3 = somewhat true, 4 = very true, and 5 = always true.

1. I have extremely high expectations for myself. 5
2. I feel that it's very important to do things just right. 4
3. Others have told me that my standards are unrealistically high. 5
4. I feel distressed if things aren't neat and in order. 3
5. I'm highly concerned about making mistakes. 5
6. I frequently doubt whether I have completed a task appropriately. 2
7. I often miss deadlines at work because I can't complete my tasks until they're just right. 1
8. It's common for me to check and recheck my work. 5
9. Some of my coworkers have told me—or implied—that I need to relax my standards. 4
10. There have been times when I've delayed team projects because I wanted to make sure that our work had no mistakes. 1
11. It's probable that my standards for work performance are significantly higher than those of most people. 5
12. A boss or coworker has told me that I tend to be inflexible about how work is done. 1

13. I'm very hard on myself if I don't excel in my work and achieve at an extremely high level. ____

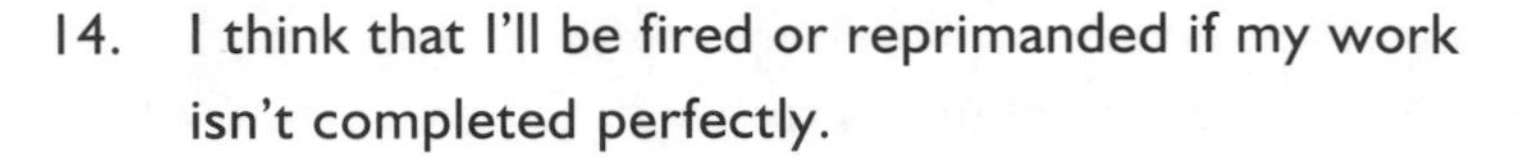

14. I think that I'll be fired or reprimanded if my work isn't completed perfectly. ____

15. I have a difficult time delegating tasks at work because I worry that the work won't get done as well as it would if I did it myself. ____

Perfectionism Quiz Scoring

If you answered mostly 4s and 5s—or had a total score higher than 55—you're likely to experience significant workplace perfectionism. This means that you most likely have several key traits of perfectionists, potentially including:

- A feeling that you need to do everything just right
- Very high standards for yourself and possibly for others
- A severe level of discomfort about the prospect of making mistakes
- An unrealistic estimation of the negative consequences of doing tasks imperfectly
- Rigid rules and guidelines for how projects need to be completed

A strong need for order and organization in your work and a lack of tolerance for disorderly activities or work spaces

Other Things Perfectionism Can Mean

Perfectionism can be linked to—or lead to—problems more significant than just a strong need to achieve. If your perfectionist behaviors reach a compulsive level or you find you're frequently depressed, angry, or anxious, it's a good idea to get a professional evaluation. Similarly, if your perfectionism is just one aspect of a set of continuous worries or you worry excessively about what others think, you may have a generalized anxiety disorder or a social anxiety disorder, respectively. Seek out a psychologist or psychiatrist who specializes in anxiety and mood disorders; they'll be able to assess whether your perfectionism is linked to something more serious than simply a desire to do things well.

Why Do I Have to Be So Perfect?

Perfectionism can be a personality trait or situational, coming and going at different points in time; it's often correlated with a high need for achievement. While we will focus specifically on how perfectionism affects your work, if you're a perfectionist—situational or otherwise—you're likely to find perfectionism in several areas of life. In an excellent book called *When Perfect Isn't Good Enough* (1998), Martin Antony identifies some of the primary areas where perfectionism is likely to come up, including:

- **Work and school performance:** e.g., doing and redoing a work task over and over
- **Neatness and aesthetics:** e.g., your house has to be perfectly color coordinated
- **Organization and ordering:** e.g., your clothes need to be folded in a particular way
- **Writing:** e.g., you need to take a long time filling out forms to be sure there is no mistake
- **Speaking:** e.g., you're very careful about not using the wrong words or mispronouncing words
- **Physical appearance:** e.g., your makeup must be applied just right or your shirt has to be pressed perfectly
- **Health and cleanliness:** e.g., you'll only eat foods that are 100 percent organic

Perfectionism as Personality

Perfectionism can become a part of your personality. One of the reasons that you're a perfectionist now is that your perfectionist behaviors have probably been rewarded in the past. As a student, your teachers may have praised and complimented you for getting good grades. You may have excelled in athletics or earned a scholarship to college at least partially as a result of your high standards. You may have heard your parents bragging to friends about how you always clean up after yourself, inspiring you to repeat the thorough cleaning all over again.

Because perfectionism is frequently rewarded and associated with success, it can easily become part of your personality. If your perfectionist behavior continues to be rewarded and reinforced, it's likely to continue and may even increase to a detrimental level.

Many girls, for example, develop eating disorders after they begin eating in a rigid manner. Initially their self-discipline is rewarded when people comment on how good they look after losing a few pounds or on how well they stick to their meal plans. This behavior is also reinforced internally, when they feel good about how they now look. Unfortunately, as a result these girls are likely to even further restrict their eating and lose weight more

coaching point

Do you have a perfectionist personality? What perfectionist tendencies have you had for most of your life? (If you're unsure, ask a parent or someone who's known you since you were young.) When something has been with you for most of your life, it's likely to be part of your personality now. In your notebook, write down all your memories of being a perfectionist. This will help you identify how long-standing and pervasive your perfectionist tendencies are.

rapidly. Thus, through being rewarded, a behavior that started out as a mild case of perfectionism can escalate into an eating disorder.

Perfectionism as a Response to a Situation

It's also possible that your perfectionism is situational and less related to your personality. You may be particularly nervous in your current job and as a result have developed some perfectionist tendencies. If you have a hypercritical boss or face a lot of professional competition, you may have simply adopted perfectionism to help you survive in your current situation.

In the case of situational perfectionism, these new characteristics may or may not be adaptive. If you're able to keep your perfectionist thoughts and behaviors from interfering with your ability to get things done, your relationships with coworkers, and your own peace of mind, then they may be working for you instead of against you.

coaching point

In your notebook, write down the times you have been perfectionistic in response to your current work situation. Then create two separate columns; label one "pros" and the other "cons." List a few ways each of your perfectionist responses has helped or hurt you, in both your career and your life.

The Demands of Today's Workplace

Standards of excellence are set by many sources: yourself, your parents, your spouse, your boss, your company. While you may set high standards for yourself, you may also be impacted by heavy demands from your work environment.

If you are someone who is prone to perfectionism and anxiety, the demands of today's workplace are likely to bring out these tendencies. As a result of intense competition between companies, businesses often pressure their employees to help the company succeed. Serious competition can also exist between employees, for promotions and bonuses; and between job applicants, to get and keep excellent positions. If you own your own business, then you most likely feel an intense pressure to do things right in order to make your business profitable. It sometimes seems as if only the perfect can survive in competitive business atmospheres.

Some of the perfectionism-related buzz words and concepts in the business world today include:

- Zero defects
- Continuous improvement
- 100 percent excellence
- Total quality management
- Right the first time and right every time

These concepts clearly imply both a demand for perfection and a low tolerance of mistakes. You may understandably fear retribution, embarrassment, or demotion if you do not complete your work with "zero defects." The stress and pressure of competitive work environments can easily lay the groundwork for perfectionism and anxiety.

Why Perfectionism = Anxiety

Since this book is about anxiety in the workplace, you're probably wondering how exactly perfectionism is related to anxiety. You probably have some ideas based on your own experiences or what we've talked about so far. Let's further explore why anxiety leads to perfectionism.

The Problems with Perfectionism

As much as thoroughness, diligence, precision, and fastidiousness may help your work performance, these characteristics can equally *hamper* your work performance—and cause anxiety. The most common work problems associated with perfectionism include inefficiency, underproduction, mental distress, and interpersonal problems with coworkers.

Time Pressure

One of the most common side effects of being exact in your work is being slower. Depending on the nature of your job, this may or may not be a problem. However, for most jobs, it is.

When you fall behind on one task, you're likely to experience a snowball effect and end up behind on several tasks. This can lead to stress—which then makes you more susceptible to anxiety—and then you need even longer to complete tasks. Unfortunately we cannot create time, it needs to come from somewhere. Many people overcompensate by taking time away from other work- or nonwork-related activities. However, when you take time away from other work tasks, you may end up letting down and frustrating your work team, preventing your boss from moving on with some of her tasks, doing a poor job on other projects, or feeling rushed and pressured to complete other activities. When you take time away from outside activities, you sacrifice hobbies, neglect your friends and family, and increase your own anxiety and stress by eliminating coping and relaxation strategies.

Lex's Story: Quality over Quantity

Lex has his own business in the technology field. Lex is the quintessential example of someone whose perfectionism has helped him to a point but also significantly hampers his professional growth. He has been able to create a successful company in a highly competitive field. His perfectionism, however, has interfered with the growth of his company because as a result of it, he's unable to do the volume of business that would make his company profitable.

Lex feels the need to oversee all of the work his staff completes. If you've ever been micromanaged, you know how irritating it is to have your boss looking over your shoulder and signing off on everything you do. Because of this, his staff does not feel empowered. Furthermore, their growth process is inhibited because Lex will often take the more complicated tasks on himself. As a result, his turnover rate is higher than other businesses in his industry.

Lex struggles with delegating tasks because he believes that his employees won't do the work as well as he could. This is often true. But it comes with heavy costs: reduced productivity and reduced employee commitment. In addition to the benefits of keeping your employees motivated and empowered, there's often a cost- benefit analysis to consider with perfectionism. Is it better to have fifty projects completed at 95 percent "perfection" or five projects completed with 100 percent "perfection"? The business world is often a numbers game and if you aren't able to produce the quantity of output, your work performance may be poor.

Worrying About Being Imperfect

As you may know, there's a high correlation between worrying and perfectionism. When you have unrealistic standards for yourself, you constantly feel like you're falling short. And when you constantly feel like you're falling short, you worry about the consequences.

Many perfectionists obsess about getting things done right. Obsessions are almost always associated with anxiety. Obsessive thought processes slow you down and keep you from focusing on the task at hand. When you obsess, you probably try to resist your obsessive thoughts—because you realize they're disruptive and anxiety-producing. Research shows that a vicious cycle results: the more you try to suppress your obsessive thoughts, the more they actually increase (Abramowitz, Tolin, and Street 2001).

If you are someone who is obsessed with meeting your own high standards, you'll probably also be anxious and fearful about how horrible it would be to fail to meet these standards. One of my clients literally believed that she would lose all esteem in the eyes of her coworkers if she made so much as a minor slip of the tongue during a presentation. As a result she spent hours preparing to be sure her presentations went smoothly. Until we worked together, she didn't realize that she could spend only a tenth of that time preparing and still give great presentations—maybe even better presentations because they no longer appeared overrehearsed.

Fearing a negative outcome because you haven't completed things perfectly is a self-perpetuating fear: it builds upon itself. As a perfectionist, it's unlikely that you typically allow yourself *not* to meet your standards. As a result, you never receive the information that not quite reaching your standards is *unlikely to be catastrophic*. This is exactly why perfectionism sticks around: you never learn that you could do fine—or possibly even better—without your perfectionist ways. Your perfectionist anxiety thus continues to feed upon itself.

Perfectionists Can Be Annoying

How do you think it comes across to others when you insist on extreme measures of diligence or exactness? On the one hand, they may admire your level of precision and care in your work. Or they may enjoy the benefits they get from you spending all of your time making your projects excellent. On the other hand, your fastidiousness may drive your supervisor, coworkers, or supervisees crazy.

The people you supervise. It's tough to have a boss who's a perfectionist—perfectionists micromanage and lack delegation skills. Perfectionist bosses are also likely to instill fear in the minds of their subordinates. If your supervisee feels that he'll never be able to complete something to your standards, he may become highly anxious and timid at work—or he may develop learned helplessness and a "why bother" attitude. Neither is conducive to a happy, motivated, productive employee.

Conflicts with coworkers. When organizations have called me in to help manage employee conflicts or conduct team-building exercises, I've frequently found perfectionism as the source of

coaching point

In your notebook, write your responses to the following questions:

1. How has perfectionism led to time pressure in your job?
2. How have you sacrificed quantity in favor of quality in an extreme manner?
3. How has your perfectionism led to worrying about negative outcomes?
4. How might you have annoyed others at work with your strictness and thoroughness?

conflict or as the limiting factor in an otherwise high-performing work team. Because they fear suboptimal performance, perfectionists are often poor at compromising.

Coworkers of perfectionists frequently feel that their points of view are either ignored or undervalued by a perfectionist team member. As a perfectionist, you're likely to be focused on your own standards for performance. If you ignore or brush aside coworkers' suggestions, they're likely to feel defensive and hostile. Then, even when you have an excellent idea or suggestion, your idea is more likely to be dismissed— because other team members feel you don't listen to their ideas. Conflict frequently brews and erupts.

The Relationship of Perfectionism, Avoidance, and Anxiety

There are extremely strong links between perfectionism, avoidance, and anxiety. Perfectionism is a form of avoidance. Perfectionism allows you to avoid the uncomfortable feelings that come along with doing things differently or in a less precise manner. Avoidance leads to anxiety. The more you avoid, the more anxious you become.

Imagine a child is bitten by a big dog. What do you think will happen if this child avoids all dogs for the next month? For six months? A year? The more you avoid, the more anxious you become.

Another aspect of avoidance that's correlated with perfectionism is an inability to distinguish between situations. If a child avoids all dogs after being bitten, he prevents himself from learning that some dogs are less dangerous than others. A small, friendly dog who is held by its owner and cheerfully licking other children is much more likely to be safe than a big stray dog roaming the streets. Yet because the child avoids all dogs, he never learns this distinction. Likewise, if you always avoid the discomfort involved in doing things imperfectly, you never learn that while it may be advantageous to do *some* things perfectly, it's unnecessary to do *everything* perfectly.

The Keys to Handling Perfectionism

I've already given away some of the tricks for dealing with perfectionism, but let's outline them step by step. At the end of each of the following sections is a coaching point or series of coaching points to help you put these ideas into practice and help you make your perfectionist tendencies work for you instead of against you.

A Reality Check

The first step to effectively dealing with perfectionism is to recognize its presence. You've probably already begun to do this just by reading through this chapter. You may, however, need to work hard to accept the idea that your perfectionism isn't always going to be beneficial; try to take a realistic look at the potential costs and benefits of letting go of your perfectionism.

You might also ask people you trust to help you with a reality check. These people could include a family member, a friend, a coach, a therapist, a colleague, a boss, or a mentor. If you're already aware of how your perfectionism is manifesting in unhelpful ways, give your support people a list of specific examples and request that they call your attention to similar behaviors to help make you aware of when you're engaging in problematic perfectionism.

Changing Your Perfect Thinking

Specific thought patterns tend to be largely responsible for perfectionism. In chapter 1, we discussed common types of thought patterns that are associated with anxiety. Many of these same thought patterns are responsible for perfectionism, which is part of why perfectionism and anxiety are closely linked. The main thought patterns that go along with perfectionism include:

All-or-None Thinking

Example: "The meeting will either go great or it will be awful."

What it means. When you engage in all-or-none thinking, your thoughts are polarized between two ends of the spectrum: fantastic and disastrous. Perfectionism tries to push you toward the extreme edge of the fantastic side of the spectrum—perfectionism makes you feel that if you move even just a little bit towards disastrous, things would be *really* disastrous.

How to change. To overcome polarized thinking you need to start seeing the gray areas. This involves looking at the possibilities that fall in the middle, between the extremes. Instead of thinking that the meeting must be either great or awful, realize that it might go well or very well. Also realize that by trying to make your work fantastic, you're wasting time and energy; attempting to push your effort from 100 percent to 150 percent doesn't work—there's no such thing as 150 percent effort!

Catastrophizing

Example: "If I don't do a perfect job on this project, my boss will regret hiring me. She'll see all of my flaws and ultimately will fire me because I didn't live up to her expectations."

What it means. As we've discussed throughout the chapter, a common occurrence in perfectionist thinking is to assume that the results of doing something imperfectly are more catastrophic than they are. This is where the importance of your reality check comes in. Some things really do need 100 percent precision or close to it. If you're a brain surgeon, even a tiny mistake can be disastrous. (However, perfectionist brain surgeons may still expect an impossible 120 percent from themselves.)

How to change. Go through your worst-case scenario in your mind, so that you understand your ultimate fear. First, ask yourself how likely that scenario truly is to happen. It's probably much less likely than you fear. Second, ask yourself how you'd handle it if it did happen. The idea here is to show yourself that even if your ultimate fear did happen (which is unlikely), you could cope with it and perhaps even turn it into something advantageous.

Selective Abstraction

Example: "I can't believe that I received a 'satisfactory' score on one of the components of my job evaluation—that is so disappointing."

What it means. This thought pattern is also known as tunnel vision. It means that you focus on a single negative—or potentially negative—piece of information and ignore all positive information. For example, you might obsess about feedback that is less than perfect but ignore the fact that most of your feedback is excellent.

One of my coaching clients gave a series of presentations to market her business. In one presentation, an audience member glared at her throughout her talk; afterwards, she received one evaluation—one out of sixteen—that described her presentation as "boring and uninteresting." Unfortunately, my client was so focused on this individual's response that she neglected to relish her fifteen positive evaluations.

How to change. Expand your vision. Look at *all* the data in a situation—the positive and the negative. When you look at the bigger picture, you gain a more realistic and often more positive view of the situation. Another strategy is to ask yourself the question, "So what?" How much does it really matter if the one detail is not perfect? Most likely, it's not important in the grand scheme of things.

Mind Reading

Example: "I just know that my boss noticed that I was underdressed and thought I didn't take the time to prepare myself. She must think I didn't take the meeting seriously."

What it means. When stuck in a mind-reading thought pattern, you're likely to make assumptions about how others are perceiving a situation. However, unless you truly have a supernatural talent, your assumptions are unlikely to be right.

How to change. Realize you can't know what's going on in someone else's head; choose instead to suspend judgment until you have specific data or evidence. For example, in the scenario above, it's equally possible that the boss thought that the man was dressed very appropriately for a casual meeting and that he presented himself well.

coaching point

Create a page in your notebook for each of the cognitive patterns described above. On each page, record all of the thoughts of the given type you had over the course of two weeks. (For example, record all of the mind-reading thoughts you had on one page, the catastrophizing thoughts on another, etc.) Then record all of the evidence for and against the particular thought being true. Finally, write down some alternative thoughts that are in line with the evidence.

Time Management

Perfectionism plays havoc with time management, because perfectionists often allocate too much time to trying to make a given project perfect. If you're able to do your projects perfectly and not get behind, you're unusually talented! For most of us, it's a challenge to juggle a busy schedule and stay on top of everything without getting behind.

coaching point

This method has worked very well for many of my busy executive clients: First, plan your work activities for several days this week (you pick which days). Next, in your notebook, divide a page into three columns. In the first column, write how much time you plan to spend on each of your major tasks. Then, in the second column, as the days pass, record how much time you actually *did* spend. This will help you see how long tasks are actually taking and where you're getting behind. In the third column, record what got you behind if a task took longer than expected or if you didn't get to a particular task.

Notice whether you were able to stick with your planned timeline and get everything done on schedule without spending too long on any one task. If you did stick with your plan, you probably needed to sacrifice some of your perfectionism to do so. What were some of the positive outcomes resulting from sticking to your timeline and sacrificing a bit of perfectionism? What were some of the outcomes when perfectionism got in the way and you were unable to do activities in the allotted time?

Prioritizing

Prioritizing is fundamental to handling perfectionism. When you approach your work as a perfectionist, everything feels like a big deal. Even tasks that appear less important to others seem important to you. Your perfectionism makes you feel like you must never make a mistake. It also produces anxiety, and anxiety frequently clouds reasoning and rational thinking abilities. A well-developed ability to prioritize is critical to overcoming perfectionism.

coaching point

Most perfectionists have organized lists of things to do. Do you have several lists of things to do? Gain practice with prioritizing your workplace tasks by putting your to-do list in order of priority. (Eventually you'll want to loosen up your standards—and list-making—but for now, let's use your list-making to our advantage.) Once you've made your list and put it in order of priority, assign times to complete each activity. You may want to get some second opinions about whether certain tasks are priorities or not—particularly if you find that more tasks are ranked as priorities than not.

As you work on prioritizing, you can also begin delegating more. Initially, it will feel easier to delegate those tasks that feel less critical. Begin with the less critical and work your way up to the more important tasks as you become more comfortable both with delegating and with others' abilities to complete the various activities.

Make More Mistakes

Here's another one of my crazy ideas! You probably think, "If making mistakes is uncomfortable to me, why should I *purposely* make a mistake?" or "Why should I make a mistake and compromise the quality of my work if I don't have to?" The answer is simple: if you never allow yourself to make minor mistakes, you never learn that perfectionism isn't always necessary.

Your Perfect Is Different

Keep in mind that what is perfect to you isn't necessarily what is perfect to all. One of my friends who is a perfectionist in her career once went on and on about how horrible a paper that she wrote was. She couldn't believe that she had submitted it after proofreading it only once. It turned out that the paper was published in a very reputable journal with only a few corrections from her initial submission. Keep this in mind: if you're a perfectionist, something that seems to be only 80 percent "perfect" by your standards is likely to be 100 percent perfect by others' standards.

Make Mistakes on Purpose

When you make a mistake on purpose, you control the type of mistake you make. Your mistake can be as simple as intentionally writing "their" instead of "there" or pronouncing something slightly wrong or tripping as you're walking into a meeting. These may sound like things you'd want to avoid doing at all costs, but when you do them, you'll learn their real consequences. You may expect that your colleagues would laugh or look at you oddly if you tripped walking down the hall. When you try it, you might find that one person asks if you are okay and no one else really seems to notice. Thus, you learn the discrepancy between your negative prediction and the actual response.

coaching point

Do this little experiment: Go through your list of prioritized activities. Pick something that is toward the middle or bottom of the list in terms of importance. Then plan a mistake to make on that activity. Write down what you fear will occur if you do the task less than perfectly or make a mistake on it. Then try to make the mistake. Record the actual response or outcome.

Keep in mind that actual outcomes may not be readily apparent. Try to choose activities for which there will be some type of immediate outcome; make your predictions about these short-term consequences. For example, instead of saying that if you pronounced something wrong in a meeting with an investor, your business will fail, predict something more specific, like you wouldn't get a contract from that investor.

Also keep in mind that there may be alternative explanations for the consequences occurring. If the investor decided not to fund your business, is it definitely because you pronounced something wrong or might there be other reasons for the investor's decision?

Perfectionism Can Work *For* You

As we've discussed in this chapter, perfectionism comes with both costs and benefits. When you use the techniques we've explored here, you can decrease the costs and help make your perfectionism work *for* you in your career.

Yet another correlate of perfectionism is being self-critical about your work performance: perfectionists are often highly skeptical about their own ability to achieve if they don't force themselves to do everything just right. We'll get into this idea more in the next chapter.

CHAPTER 4

Your Own Worst Enemy

"You don't have to fear defeat if you believe it can reveal powers that you didn't know you possessed."

—NAPOLEON HILL

When You Are Your Harshest Critic

In the last chapter, we discussed how perfectionism can be problematic. It can be annoying and frustrating—both for you and for others who may be affected by your perfectionist ways.

Whether or not you're a perfectionist, you may have a problem with self-criticism. Perfectionists are critical about work they feel is less than perfect. People who are self-critical may be similarly critical—either because they're perfectionists, or because they lack confidence, compare themselves harshly to others, or fail to recognize their own accomplishments. The major area of overlap between unhealthy self-criticism and perfectionism is having excessively high standards for yourself. The result? You guessed it: anxiety.

When you're your own worst enemy, who's your strongest advocate? Who supports you, who cheers you on, who celebrates your accomplishments?

Even if you're fortunate enough to have someone who *does* advocate for you and support you, if you want to have a successful and enjoyable career, this won't be enough. To be most effective and most believable, positive feedback needs to come from *you*.

Your thoughts shape your reality. If you constantly doubt yourself, your fears will eventually become self-fulfilling, no matter how many great things another says. And what if the person cheering you on isn't around? Who will do it then?

Relying on someone else to give you positive feedback is simply neither effective nor practical. Plus, if you aren't able to recognize your accomplishments yourself, you won't truly believe the positive encouragement another gives you. Have you ever had a day when you felt you looked particularly awful? Maybe you couldn't get your hair to look okay, or your shirt was wrinkled, or your outfit just didn't look right. If someone then tells you that you look very nice, do you suddenly feel like you look great? Their compliment may make you feel a bit better, but if you're already sure you look awful, the compliment will quickly be dismissed as inaccurate.

Self-Defeating Thinking

Certain thought patterns are hurtful and not helpful to you. With self-criticism, you may think that you're giving yourself constructive feedback, but really you're just giving yourself a hard time.

Jon's Story: Thoughts That Harm

My client Jon had a problem with self-defeating thought patterns. As he sat on the train on the way home from work every day, he would mentally review all of the things that he'd done—or not done—during the day that he wasn't pleased about. He'd think: "I didn't finish that report. I left a stack of work on my desk. I didn't present myself very well during the meeting with the people from marketing. I forgot to ask Larry about the changes to the budget . . ." His list went on and on. He'd then focus on all of the difficulties he'd encounter the next day as a result. "My team won't have the information they need to do the budget properly. I'll be behind on everything. I'll let my boss down . . ." Another endless list.

Clearly Jon's thoughts were self-defeating—he'd dwell on perceived flaws but entirely overlook the things he was actually doing very well. Jon had become trapped in a problematic thought pattern: by focusing on negatives and overlooking positives, he set himself up to only create more negatives.

It may be easy to spot problematic thought patterns with someone else—in this case, Jon—but can you do it for yourself?

In his best-selling book *The Attractor Factor* (2005), author Joe Vitale discusses how to attract success to you. One way he recommends is to focus on living success. What you focus on expands. If you focus on what you lack, he says, you'll attract more of what you lack. If you focus on your failures, you'll attract more failure. On the other hand, if you focus on your successes, you'll attract more success.

Focusing on the negative leads to anxiety. It's nerve-wracking to have all of your attention focused on what you're doing wrong. As a result, more mistakes and failures then occur. It's another vicious cycle: because what you're focusing on (the negative) is expanding, you become even more nervous and focus on it even more.

Do You Suffer from Self-Doubt?

Another common form self-defeating thought patterns take in the workplace is self-doubt: You question your abilities. You find it difficult to be self-assured in your work performance and interactions with others. You tell yourself to play it safe. You avoid all risks.

Some people experience just a little bit of self-doubt, while others experience a great deal. Even a small amount of self-doubt can be problematic: it can prevent you from making the critical decisions necessary to take your career to a whole new level. Moving forward takes courage and typically involves some risk. If you doubt your abilities, second-guess yourself, or let fear control you, you may stay in place or go backwards, but it's unlikely you'll ever move forward.

Self-doubt frequently leads to counterproductive excuses. For example, if you need to do something that requires you to use a software program that is new to you, you may tell yourself, "I can't do that—I don't know how." Is this really true or is it an excuse? Do you really not know how to use the software? If you don't, couldn't you learn?

I found myself making these types of excuses a while back when I needed to use the program QuickBooks for my business accounting. I told myself that I didn't know how to use it and I doubted my abilities to learn it, given that I'm not particularly technology savvy. However, at long last I decided to put an end to the excuses and figure out how to use the program. It was so self-explanatory that I learned it in an afternoon. I couldn't believe I'd let my doubt and excuses hold me back!

In their best-selling book *Rich Dad, Poor Dad* (2000), authors Robert T. Kiyosaki and Sharon L. Lechter write:

> We all have tremendous potential, and we are all blessed with gifts. Yet, the one thing that holds all of us back is some degree of self-doubt. It is not so much the lack of technical information that holds us back, but more the lack of confidence. (110)

Although they're discussing self-doubt in relation to financial intelligence, just as self-doubt holds you back from financial intelligence and wealth, it also holds you back from soaring ahead in your career.

Whether you own a business or not, the ability to take calculated risks is critical to advancing your career and accumulating wealth. Don't let self-doubt hold you back! You'll never learn what

coaching point

Make a list, either of little things that you're afraid of or of small steps toward something new and bold. On your calendar, assign items from your list to every single day of the next month. At the end of your month, ask yourself whether you learned anything. Try to learn from the fact that you actually *did* these things, not necessarily from their outcomes. Confidence can grow simply from trying something challenging, regardless of how it turns out.

you're truly capable of if you don't go for it. Two surefire strategies for tackling self-doubt (and the anxiety it brings) at work are:

- Do something you are afraid of every day
- Make bold, courageous decisions

The more you face your anxiety, the less doubt you will have—now that's win-win!

Harsh Comparisons to Others

I'm sure that there have been times when you've compared yourself to your coworkers. We've all done this. It's human nature to look at the performance of others and question how you measure up. In fact, it can be a very beneficial thing to do—this is one of the ways that we grow in our work. If we see someone outperforming us, we can learn from their accomplishments; we can become inspired to push ourselves harder.

Of course, too much of a good thing turns it into definitely not a good thing. This is always the case with anxiety. A moderate amount of anxiety can give us energy, motivation, and drive, but at a certain point anxiety begins to negatively affect us and those around us.

Obviously, if you continuously compare yourself to your colleagues and think about how much better, smarter, more attractive, more efficient, or more productive they are, you'll feel bad. Taken to the extreme, these types of social comparisons can make you feel depressed, hopeless, and socially anxious.

We'll delve further into the problem of social anxiety— being nervous around others—in chapter 9. For now, recognize that regularly comparing yourself to others in a way that puts yourself down is likely to both increase your discomfort and decrease your work performance.

Overlooking Your Accomplishments

In the case study described earlier, Jon was very good at recognizing all of the things he didn't do, all of the things he didn't do well, and all of the potential problems that might arise as a result. If his job were to be a critic of himself, he'd be getting promotions and raises all over the place. But as it was, his overly critical thought patterns held him back from enjoying and excelling in his career.

While Jon was great at acknowledging what he did wrong, he wasn't very good at acknowledging what he did *right*. But if Jon doesn't notice what he's doing well, how's he supposed to keep doing the things he does well? And how is he going to promote himself in his job?

If you don't know what you're doing right, you'll not only feel like you're underperforming, you'll also be unable to capitalize on your strengths and accomplishments. And if you're not able to effectively promote yourself, decision makers won't realize just how great you are and how much they need to promote you.

Many professionals I have spoken to and coached tell me that they fear that if they stop keeping themselves in check with self-criticism they'll become arrogant—or come across to others as arrogant. Do you have this concern? Do you feel like maybe it's a good thing that you criticize yourself because it helps you keep yourself from becoming smug?

This is a very common fear with anxiety. People often want to keep anxiety around so it can keep them in line. For this reason, self-defeating thinking can be difficult to give up. Even while part of you realizes that it's not helpful, part of you may still think it is. It's like the coach who yells and screams at his team members. Unless the coach is truly a nasty person, he probably believes his yelling and screaming is helpful—he may even feel that he can scare them into shaping up.

Studies show otherwise. Decades of research on motivating behavioral changes show that positive reinforcement is the best way to achieve behavioral changes. With positive reinforcement you increase a desired behavior's frequency by rewarding it.

Punishing an undesired behavior to decrease its frequency tends to be less effective.

This is true for all kinds of behaviors. For example, if you're housebreaking a dog (as I am right now), it's much more effective to reward and praise him when he relieves himself outside than to scold him when he goes inside. Similarly, if you want your children to get good grades, it's more powerful to compliment great test scores than to yell about bad test scores. The same goes for your work performance. If you want to perform fantastically, it's important to notice all the little things you're doing right and reward yourself for them.

If you're nervous about appearing arrogant, remember this: people are naturally very perceptive; we can tell who really is— and isn't—arrogant. The people who come across as arrogant are the ones who *are* arrogant. (And if you really are arrogant, know that you can still change.) You can be confident without being arrogant—and people are highly attracted to confidence.

It's Time to Stop Being Your Own Enemy

So what does Jon need to do differently to transform himself from his own worst critic into his own best advocate? Jon could practice the following steps—and so can you.

Self-Promoting Thinking

In contrast to self-defeating thinking, self-promotional thinking helps you to both develop a more realistic understanding of your own strengths and weaknesses and use these strengths and weaknesses to your advantage. The first step is to become aware of your self-defeating thought patterns. Then you can work to understand them differently and learn from them. This will help you control these thoughts—rather than allowing them to control you.

coaching points

1. In your notebook, at the end of each day record your thoughts about the day. Do this for several days. Don't try to do anything differently at this point. We just want to see how your thoughts are operating.
2. After you've collected several days' worth of data on your thoughts, sort them out by placing each thought into one of three columns: very true (almost 100 percent accurate), somewhat true (around 50 percent accurate), or not true (less than 10 percent accurate). This will help you see that the original thoughts may have been overly harsh and not accurate. Additionally, remember: even if they are accurate, they may not actually be problematic or a big deal.
3. The third step is to proactively work on the truly problematic situations that end up in the very true category (and make sure that all of your thoughts don't end up in this column). Now you can actually use your self-criticism constructively, by focusing on a few important things that you can be proactive about rather than on tons of negative—and sometimes inconsequential—things.

Self-Promoting Actions

In addition to identifying the few important problems that do need to be addressed, you also want to take action steps to help you both stop beating yourself up and promote yourself.

coaching points

1. The first step is to realize why you aren't recognizing your successes. What are you afraid of? Write these things down. Then, test these out as predictions and hypotheses. For example, let's say that you write, "I'm afraid I'll come across as overly arrogant if I don't criticize myself to keep myself humble." Then you give up your self-criticism and see what happens. Do people respond differently to you? Do they treat you like you're acting arrogantly? What evidence do you have that you really come across as conceited without the self put-downs?
2. The next step is to start recognizing your successes. It's easy to let the little successes slip by and focus instead on all that wasn't done or wasn't done well. Stop this from happening by keeping a success inventory: at the end of each day, write down all of the accomplishments of the day. They don't need to be related to your career and they can be things as small as "I got my grocery shopping done and saved nine dollars with coupons." A successful life makes a successful career; write down any accomplishments you can think of.

coaching points

(continued)

3. Notice how you feel as you start to become more aware of your achievements. Does it motivate you? Do you feel more inspired? You probably will find yourself both motivated and inspired. Because success builds upon itself like a snowball, you're likely to become energized and motivated by this process.
4. If not, think about why not. Are you nervous about something? Reluctant to change your ways? Fearful that you'll set yourself up for a letdown? Record your concerns, but keep testing yourself and practicing the behaviors in question; most likely you'll see that the fears don't come to fruition.
5. Create and implement a plan to do what makes you uncomfortable. It's fine to start small, as long as you push yourself in the direction of doing what feels uncomfortable. If it makes you feel odd to describe your accomplishments to your team, try it. If you're nervous and unsure about giving up your self-criticism, do it. The key is: *know what you're uncomfortable about—and then do it anyway*. You'll likely gain comfort, courage, and confidence.
6. In *Feeling Good: The New Mood Therapy* (1980), author David Burns recommends that you "test your can'ts." The idea is to put the pessimistic, self-defeating thoughts to the test and see if they

coaching points

(continued)

are really right. Conduct some experiments and find out if you really can't do something. To do this, pick a task at work that you've been putting off by saying that you can't do it. Then break it up into small steps. Try the first step. If it turns out to be too big of a step, break it down and try it again. Likely you'll find out that you really can accomplish the task that you thought you couldn't.

Comparing Your Comparisons

Comparing yourself to your coworkers can be helpful if done right—but it's rarely done right. Here's how to use social comparisons successfully and healthily:

coaching points

1. In your notebook, record the ways that you compare yourself harshly to your coworkers or boss. For example, "As I was listening to Maria's presentation, I thought about how calm and poised she is and how awful I'll seem presenting after her since I am a horrible presenter."

coaching points

(continued)

2. Note which parts of your comparison are helpful and which are not. For example, "Thinking that I'll look awful compared to Maria just made me feel more nervous. Thinking that I'm horrible at presenting made me insecure about standing up to talk. Realizing that she's calm and poised made me feel good because it shows that it's possible to appear calm and come across well while presenting."
3. Next, look for other ways to utilize the information in your comparison. Given the fact that much of the comparison isn't helpful, how can you rework it? For example, "Using the audio-visual materials made Maria look very professional and knowledgeable. I too can use those materials in that way. Maybe I think I'm coming across much worse than I actually do. I could compliment Maria on her presentation and ask her for feedback on mine to help me improve."

When You Lack Confidence About Speaking

One of the most common things that people criticize themselves harshly about in the workplace is public speaking. If this sounds like you, read on!

CHAPTER 5

When You Want to Stay Quiet

> "All of us are born with a set of instinctive fears—of falling, of the dark, of lobsters, of falling on lobsters in the dark, or speaking before a Rotary Club, and of the words "Some Assembly Required.""
>
> —DAVE BARRY

The Very Common Fear of Public Speaking

> Do you hate the feeling of being in the spotlight?
>
> Does your heart race, or do you feel out of breath or shaky when you have to give a presentation?
>
> Do you experience performance anxiety when answering questions in the boardroom?
>
> Would you rather be anywhere else instead of speaking in front of people?
>
> Does the prospect of needing to answer questions spontaneously make you uncomfortable?

If you answered yes to any of these questions, then this chapter can help you! Anxiety about public speaking is not only common, it's thought to be the greatest fear most people face. Comic Jerry Seinfeld is quoted as saying, "At a funeral, most people would rather be the one in the casket than the one giving the eulogy."

So, if speaking up at work bothers you, know that you are not alone. However, although you may want to stay quiet, if you don't want your work to suffer you can't.

As with any form of anxiety, some phobias and fears fall within a "normal" range—they don't cause clinically significant impairment. However, if your fear of public speaking is creating extreme levels of anxiety or significant impairment, then it's a good idea to seek an evaluation from a cognitive behavioral psychologist specializing in anxiety disorders (see the back of the book for referral sources).

In this chapter, we'll look at different types of speaking situations and identify what specifically makes you nervous and what you can do about it. Let's begin by looking at spontaneous speaking situations.

Spontaneous Speech

When you're uncomfortable in situations during which you'll need to say something on the spur of the moment, there are many potential concerns. You may be afraid that you'll say something stupid. Or you may feel like you'll blank out and have nothing to say. Or you may be concerned that you'll say the wrong thing—or even just that you'll have a sudden rush of anxiety that will be visible to others.

When physical symptoms of anxiety accompany speaking in public, people often worry about how horrible the symptoms feel, whether people can see the symptoms, and whether the symptoms will interfere with the ability to speak eloquently. In spontaneous speech situations, the symptoms often come on very quickly, whereas in planned speaking situations (e.g., a rehearsed speech), symptoms build over time.

Think about which physical signs and symptoms come up for you when you speak in public. Here are some of the common physical symptoms associated with anxiety about public speaking:

- Feeling flushed or hot
- A racing or pounding heart
- Breathlessness or shallow breathing
- Feeling dizzy or light-headed
- Sweating
- Shaky or trembling hands
- Blushing
- Upset stomach, gastrointestinal distress
- Blurred vision

Think of the last time that you were called upon to say something when you weren't ready for it. What concerned you in that situation? What physical symptoms did you experience? What was the situation? Let's explore some of the common situations during which anxiety about spontaneous speaking occurs.

Sue's Story: Impromptu Presentations

When one of my clients, Sue, suddenly had to give an impromptu presentation, she became highly anxious. Sue was sitting in a meeting and a coworker was giving a presentation on a topic that they had researched together. Sue had used some of the research on another project which she was just in the midst of wrapping up. When her coworker finished his presentation, their boss said, "Sue, didn't you find some interesting related issues? Why don't you present what you've found so far?"

Sue froze. Her mind went blank; she was unable to remember any of the information from her project. Part of the problem was that she hadn't yet synthesized the information in her own mind. But the other part of the problem was that she greatly disliked impromptu speaking.

Her nerves got the better of her: she was unable to describe her fascinating project. Instead, Sue just muttered something quickly and then invented an excuse about being late to a meeting with a client and left. This incident prompted her to contact me.

What do you think was one of the first changes I worked on with Sue? If you're thinking that I had her commit to not avoid speaking situations, you're right. In this instance, the combination of her excuse and her avoidance made her seem much less competent than she would have seemed if she had only stayed in the situation and done her best.

Presentations are often nerve-wracking, even for those who are used to giving them—and they become that much more difficult when you don't have a chance to prepare ahead of time.

Speaking Up in the Boardroom

Another spontaneous speech situation at work that often causes anxiety is the boardroom meeting. Boardroom meetings are often associated with a great deal of pressure. You may be face to face with the company CEO. If it's your own company you may be meeting with investors who are going to grill you to see if your company is worth investing in. Regardless of the purpose of the meeting, it can be difficult to both speak up and stand up for yourself.

Because it's difficult to know the content of the conversation and therefore how to prepare, you might be tempted to stay quiet. Or you might try to make the situation less spontaneous by planning out what you're going to say, so that you hopefully have something to offer by the time the conversation comes around to you.

Stakes are often higher in the boardroom—and anxiety thrives when stakes are high. Later in the chapter you'll learn how to handle the anxiety and gain confidence in the pressure-filled boardroom.

Answering Questions

Have you ever had someone ask you a question at work—and had no idea how to respond? Have you ever been caught off guard with a question in front of colleagues? If so, you know that horrible feeling of all eyes being on you as you try to figure out how to answer. Questions are so anxiety-provoking because you aren't the one in control—you don't know what will be asked of you and you don't know whether you'll even know the answer or at least have a decent response.

You may find that questions in certain contexts are more difficult to deal with than in others. Some people fear the question-and-answer sections of presentations—they do fine with the formal presentation but freeze up when the unstructured questions start coming their way. Others worry about informal watercooler conversations at work in which they're asked questions about their lives.

Doing interviews with the media can be very intimidating when you don't know the questions ahead of time, particularly when you're live. Well, you're live at work every day! Unless you have somehow arranged to collect questions ahead of time, questions are spontaneous and unpredictable. It feels like you have no control.

Sales Dialogues

Sales conversations can be a particularly difficult type of question situation, because you're asking for someone's business. If you're in sales or have ever been, you know how tough it can be to close the sale and ask for the purchase.

Salespeople often experience anxiety in very particular ways at work. Common areas of anxiety include a fear of offending someone or being pushy, concerns about cold calling, worrying about making sales numbers, distress about saying things in the right way to earn a sale, and nervousness about giving sales presentations.

Most of the salespeople I've worked with are particularly concerned about the conclusion of the sales dialogue, when it's time to close the deal. People in sales often feel uncomfortable doing this, or feel like they don't know how to best ask the necessary questions. There's usually a lot on the line at this point in the process, so it can be extremely anxiety-provoking to feel that you have to ask a pointed question to land the project or account.

I include this discussion about sales dialogues in this section on spontaneous speaking because when done right a sales dialogue has spontaneous elements, from both sides of the conversation. Sales dialogues present a tricky challenge: on the one hand, you need to be at least somewhat spontaneous so you don't come across as giving a canned speech; on the other hand, the person or people you're speaking to will likely have a lot of questions of their own, so you need to be prepared. The key is to be prepared without being overly rehearsed. We all know salespeople who sound like robots—you don't want to be one of them.

The Review

Another spontaneous speech situation at work that you may find anxiety-provoking is your annual review (or other meetings in which your supervisor gives you feedback). Being reviewed can be intimidating; again, it's an important meeting but you don't know what your supervisor will say and you don't know how you'll have to respond.

If being evaluated by your supervisor causes you discomfort, ask yourself whether it's the negative feedback or the positive feedback that makes you more uncomfortable. Some people don't know what to say when they are given positive feedback, so while it's nice to hear positive comments, it can feel awkward. Others worry about getting evaluated negatively and fear that they'll have to come up with something to say on the spot to defend themselves.

Planned Speaking Situations

If the situations described above don't sound like you but you do experience speaking anxiety, your anxiety may be linked instead to public speaking in planned speaking situations.

Giving Presentations

The formality of a planned talk can make you feel strange. This is especially true if you don't give a lot of formal talks—it can take time to become comfortable giving them. One common concern in situations where you must—or choose to—memorize your speech is that you may forget important parts of it.

Another common concern is that you'll give your presentation or speech either too quickly or too slowly. As you may know from your own personal experience, when you're nervous it's easy to make a talk too long or too short. Many anxious speakers end a talk quickly or rush through it just to get it over with. Others,

coaching point

First, write down all of the ways in which your speaking anxiety comes up at work. Recognize whether spontaneous speaking or planned speeches are more difficult for you. Second, write down all of the things that you do in those situations to try to perform better. This list should include whatever you may do to try to reduce your anxiety or make your nervousness less visible to others. Pay attention to which of these things seem to help and which do not.

fearful of forgetting something important, or hoping they'll touch on a great point, end up rambling on and on.

Leading Workshops

Workshops present another type of challenge: they're both planned and interactive. There's an art to leading effective workshops, because they require that you both interact with people individually and impart information through your presentation.

Because of this, workshops are actually in between planned and spontaneous speeches: you plan what you are going to say, but you don't always know how your workshop participants will react and what *they'll* say.

I've had the experience of leading an exercise in a workshop that was supposed to produce an exciting "aha!" moment but flopped. The conclusion that I expected never got made, so I had to think on my feet to come up with some interesting way to pull it all together. The funny thing was that I had done that exercise in previous workshops and previously it had always worked well. With workshops, you never know exactly what will happen. Much of it depends on the nature and culture of the group you're working with.

Another difficulty with workshops is, again, having to spontaneously answer questions. Because workshops are typically quite interactive, audience members are free to ask you questions. Sometimes you even get a hostile or challenging audience member who seems to actively want to throw you for a loop. If you weren't anxious already, you're sure to be now!

Now that we've addressed some of the situations in which speaking anxiety can occur, we're going to move on to the good part: how to beat it. But first, let's be sure that you know how speaking anxiety comes up at work for you.

The Keys to Change

Various scientific studies have found certain strategies successful in overcoming fears about speaking in public and concerns about being negatively evaluated by others. Ready to do away with your fears about public speaking? If so, read on to learn how to apply these studies to your life.

Focus of Attention

You enter the room where you're about to give a presentation in front of your entire department. You're thinking, "I hope I don't make a fool of myself!" and feeling like there's a good chance that you might. Your heart rate speeds up and you feel yourself starting to sweat. Your hands begin to tremble. You put on your jacket to hide the sweating and try to figure out how to position yourself so people won't see the trembling of your hands.

As all of this is happening, what are you focused on? Most likely, your focus is on *you.* But scrutinizing yourself will only make you feel increasingly self-conscious. As a result, you'll now become even more highly aware of your thoughts, your physical responses to the anxiety, and your behaviors.

Try this simple experiment: Focus all of your attention on an itch on the tip of your nose. It feels like someone is tickling your nose with a feather. Be highly aware of this itchy, tickling sensation. Notice your desire to scratch the itch. What happens? If you really focused all of your attention on this imaginary itch, you probably actually feel an itch now, even though it wasn't there to begin with. Our minds are quite good at increasing that which is in our awareness; if we're focusing on our anxiety—or the components of it—we will feel even more anxious as a result.

So, when you're faced with a speaking situation—whether it be spontaneous or planned—remember that the focus of your attention can affect the intensity of your anxiety. Focus outward.

coaching points

1. Do some further experiments to see how your focus on yourself increases your anxiety. Purposefully focus on yourself and then observe your reactions. Then purposefully focus *externally* and see what happens. For example, you could try walking through a high traffic area in your office twice. The first time, focus entirely on yourself, including your own thoughts and physical feelings. The second time, keep your focus entirely external, on all of the sights and sounds of your office. Which makes you feel more self-conscious?
2. Next, begin to train your focus of attention so you're able to focus outward in various speaking situations. Do this by practicing first in situations that don't involve high stakes. Just as you

coaching points

(continued)

wouldn't wait to begin practicing your baseball swing until the day of a huge game, you don't want to wait to practice retraining your attention until you're in the midst of a difficult speaking situation.

3. Think of yourself as a camera, focusing on everything around you. If a camera focused on itself and not its subjects, it would never get an accurate picture of the world around it. Likewise, your focus on your anxiety can cloud your ability to judge a situation realistically, making you see criticisms and judgments that aren't really there.
4. To train yourself to focus externally, pick a few everyday activities (doing the dishes, walking your dog, driving to work, etc.) and focus all of your attention and energy on whatever you're doing. Be mindful of what's happening at the moment. Use your five senses to take in information from your environment.
5. Don't try to *not* focus on yourself—that can make you even more focused on yourself! Instead, practice focusing externally (Clark 2001).

Compensating Behaviors

If you're like most people with anxiety about public speaking, there are probably certain behaviors that you rely on to help you feel like you are coming across better when you are speaking (Clark 2001). These may include:

- Trying to make your anxiety unnoticeable or less noticeable to others
- Trying to feel less nervous
- Trying to improve your performance

Do you notice a theme in the bulleted points listed above? How about the phrase "trying to?" I intentionally used this phrase because although these behaviors are designed to help you, in reality they often hurt you.

Let's say that you watch someone named Avi give a presentation. Avi is a very nervous public speaker and he's concerned about his sweating, his blushing, and the trembling of his hands. So to hide his sweating—and the blushing on his neck—he wears a dark-colored turtleneck sweater; to try to disguise the trembling of his hands, he keeps them tightly clamped together or hides them behind the screen of his laptop.

Can you picture why these behaviors would be wrong? Compensatory strategies—or "safety behaviors"—which are meant to keep you feeling comfortable tend to actually be more observable to the audience than the feared behaviors would have been in the first place. For example, our audience probably noticed Avi's big sweater. And although the sweater might conceal the blushing on Avi's neck and the sweating around his armpits, it also may have created additional facial blushing and sweating. Similarly, Avi's decision to tightly grip his hands will make his hand muscles even more tense, thus making them that much more likely to shake. Moreover, because he was trying to make the trembling of his hands less noticeable, he probably also used his hands noticeably awkwardly.

Thus, safety behaviors actually make your anxiety more visible. Although they're supposed to disguise signs of anxiety, they often call attention to them by making your behavior seem forced, contrived, unnatural, or odd.

And what happens to you when you're trying so hard to hide your trembling hands? Where does your attention go? Onto your hands and yourself. And as you now know, self-focused attention typically only increases anxiety and self-consciousness.

Here are some of the most common compensatory or safety behaviors associated with speaking in public, why they don't work, and how to change them:

Mental Rehearsal

Do you ever plan what you're going to say in your head? Think about the right way to say something while someone else is talking? Think about how you'll present something long before it's your turn to present?

Mentally rehearsing your words before you say them is a common safety behavior. But this is one of those behaviors that clearly backfires, and only ends up increasing anxiety. As you are planning what you'll say, what are you listening to? Are you focused on the conversation—or audience—or yourself?

While it's certainly helpful to consider what you're going to say before you say it, overrehearsal is likely to come at a great cost. People will feel that you aren't paying attention to them—and legitimately so. Moreover, your statements will sound overly rehearsed.

One of the main problems with mental rehearsal is that it automatically increases self-focused attention, which then increases nervousness and impairs how you come across to others. The best way to relinquish this safety behavior is to practice speaking spontaneously. Say whatever pops into your head. When you pair this practice with increasing your external-focused attention, you'll find that you're now paying close attention to your interactions with others. As a result, your response will automatically be relevant.

Trying to Hide Physical Symptoms

When you speak in public, you may feel like you're in a spotlight and every physical symptom you experience is highly obvious. Physical aspects people commonly want to hide include blushing and flushing, trembling, sweating, shaking, facial twitches, awkward hand gestures and body postures, and physical features that they feel are unattractive.

If you have concerns about physical aspects, the best thing to do is be as natural as possible. Remember that the more you attempt to hide, the more is revealed. Don't stand behind a podium like a statue. Don't cake on the makeup to hide blushing. Don't cross your arms to conceal a large midsection. Be yourself, connect with those whom you're speaking with or to, and don't try to conceal things that probably aren't even obvious in the first place.

Trying to Sound Smart

Along with trying to say things well by mentally rehearsing them, people with anxiety about public speaking often worry that they'll appear unintelligent or stupid. If you worry about this, you may attempt to sound smart by selecting big words, saying things very thoughtfully, or trying to sound knowledgeable about the topic at hand even if you aren't.

For people with this safety behavior, answering questions offers an additional challenge: because you want to sound like an authority, it can be hard to confess that you don't know an answer. You may fumble your way through your answers. You may ramble. And as a result, you may come across much worse than you would have if you'd simply said you weren't sure but would get back to the person.

Have you ever witnessed someone trying to sound intelligent? They throw in a lot of fancy words—but use them wrong. They have an arrogant air about them. Their attempt to sound intelligent certainly *doesn't* draw you to them or make you like them!

The solution? If you don't know an answer, just say so. Don't try to talk about something beyond your knowledge or experience. Even at work in a high-stakes conversation or presentation, speak as though you're talking to a good friend. If you notice that you're trying to sound intelligent, stop! Clearly you are intelligent enough to be in the job that you are in. If you seem to be trying too hard to prove yourself, it will seem like you're trying to hide something.

Avoiding Speaking Situations

This is the biggest and most damaging safety behavior. You figure: I can't possibly make a fool of myself if I don't do any public speaking. Wrong! (Well, you may be able to avoid making a fool of yourself, but you're also most likely putting your career at a serious disadvantage.)

The more you avoid doing something, the harder it becomes to do it. Likewise, the best way to get over anxiety about doing something is to do it over and over again. Imagine that you watch a horrifying movie; the movie scares you to death and as a result you have nightmares every night. Now imagine that you watch the same movie every day for two weeks straight. What would happen at the end of the two weeks? Would you still be scared of the movie? Most likely not. In fact, by this point you might actually find it silly, boring, or amusing. As we've already discussed, we naturally habituate to anxiety-provoking things over time.

You may be thinking that you've had many experiences of speaking that caused anxiety and yet you are still nervous about it. If this is so, the culprit is likely to be either self-focused attention or safety behaviors. Both of these factors maintain anxiety and interfere with the process of habituation.

Is It Really That *Bad?*

Studies have shown that people have a tendency to overestimate the consequences of making a mistake in a social situation (Foa et al. 1996). We think that a speaking faux pas will lead to significant scrutiny, judgments, or negative consequences for our careers. In reality, outcomes tend to be much less catastrophic—for example, typically, not only will people quickly forget an unfavorable speaking situation, you'll also have plenty more chances to make a good impression.

coaching point

Think about the last time that you assumed something horrible would result from a speaking situation. What did you think would happen? Try to remember all the catastrophic outcomes you imagined, such as, "My coworkers won't want to associate with me," "I could lose my job," and so on.

Now think about which of those fears actually came true. Did your coworkers really disengage from you? Did you end up losing your job because of your speaking mistake? Chances are, you'll see that the fears are much worse than the reality. Realizing this can help take the pressure off speaking—and let you feel much more relaxed.

Speaking with Confidence

To sum up, the three keys to overcoming speaking anxiety are:

1. Speak in public in the types of spontaneous or planned speaking situations that make you nervous *as much as possible*. Seek out opportunities both at work and outside of work to confront your fear—and do it over and over again.
2. When you do speak, focus externally on the conversation or the audience. Use your senses to take in information and objectively and accurately look at the situation.
3. Drop any safety behaviors which may be maintaining your anxiety, making you perform worse than you would otherwise, or making your anxiety symptoms more obvious.

coaching points

Make a list of the situations in which you can practice the specific types of speaking that you're presently uncomfortable with. For example, if you're nervous about giving planned speeches, join a Toastmasters group (see www.toastmasters.org). If you find meeting new colleagues nerve-wracking, attend a networking group where you meet new people each time.

Once you've made your list, rank the situations on it from least difficult to most difficult. Begin with the least difficult situations. Do them until they are no longer anxiety-producing; then advance to more difficult situations.

If you have a trusted friend, boss, or colleague at work, ask them for some feedback about how you come across in speaking situations. Most likely you come across better than you think. Just because you *feel* anxious doesn't mean you look anxious or are unable to perform well. This is why we often rate our performances worse than others do: we're influenced by how nervous we felt in the situation. Getting feedback from others can help you to see this. It can also give you some realistic pointers about things you can do differently.

Now that you have the tools to speak with confidence at work, get out there and begin getting experience! Over time, you're sure to see the difference.

CHAPTER 6

The Fear of Failure That Leads to Failure

"The greatest barrier to success is the fear of failure."

—SVEN-GÖRAN ERIKSSON

Uncovering a Fear of Defeat

Do you ever feel paralyzed by your fear of doing something wrong? Do you worry that you will feel horrible if you attempt something and fail? Does it feel better to not try at all than to try and fail?

If you find yourself thinking things like, "I shouldn't take that project on because I won't do well on it," or "There's no way I can handle all of the responsibilities of this new position," then you may be controlled by a fear of failure. Many people are afraid that they'll give their all to their work and still not cut it. The idea that you don't have what it takes is a hard one to stomach. However, this fear of failure can cause you to not push yourself appropriately and not take enough risks. The result is reduced levels of success and confidence.

Some of the common situations at work that bring up a fear of failure include:

- Trying something new
- Accepting a promotion
- Giving it your all
- Not giving it your all

Let's go through these one at a time.

New things—a new project, role, work team, coworkers, boss, etc.—can be very intimidating. This is because you don't already have a history of successfully handling the particular situation. As a result, you're likely to worry about your performance and fear that you'll fail or underperform.

Accepting a promotion is a specific type of trying something new—you're accepting a different work role. If you have or have had this concern, you probably felt ridiculous for having it. For most people, a work promotion is a highly sought after goal. However, when you're nervous about failing in a new role, a promotion can create a great dilemma: On the one hand, there are usually wonderful benefits associated with a promotion, like increased responsibility and pay. On the other hand, you may have to do things which make you very uncomfortable, like lead people. (We'll talk more about leadership in chapter 10.)

You probably wondered why the last two items on the list are opposites of each other. This actually illustrates how funny anxiety is—it's often one extreme or the other. When you're afraid of giving something your all, part of you fears that you have the possibility of failing even if you do give it your all and you don't want to find out that this is true. You may be someone who subscribes to the idea that what you don't know doesn't hurt you—you'd rather not know that you can't cut it. So you give under 100 percent. This way, even if you do fail, you can say that it's okay because you weren't *really* trying.

On the flip side is the fear that if you give anything under 100 percent, you'll be likely to fail. As you can probably guess, this idea is driven by perfectionism. As a result, giving your work anything less than your all is nerve-wracking.

Why You Have This Fear

There are many reasons that you may be nervous about failing in your career. The following are some of the main causes of this fear:

A Learned Worry

Many fears are learned from your environment. There are several ways that you can learn to be afraid of failure. For example, you may have learned it from witnessing someone close to you worrying a lot about bad things happening—perhaps as a child you heard your mother or father express a lot of concern about something horrible resulting from their actions or inactions. As a result of what you've observed, your brain starts to connect risks and important situations with anxiety. You expect a negative result and feel like you need to work to make sure it doesn't occur. Thus, through witnessing the worrying of others, you learn to fear failure yourself.

Another way you can learn to fear failure is to be around people who are highly critical. These people often either imply or directly tell you that you'll fail. They'll respond to your failures with an attitude of "yeah, we expected that." But they respond to your successes with "you got lucky this time." Which brings us to the next point . . .

Your Attributions for Success and Failure

Over time, we develop ways to explain our successes and failures. One of these is our *locus of control.* Locus of control is a concept developed by Julian Rotter in 1966; it describes how you expect results and reinforcement to occur.

External Locus of Control

If you have an external locus of control, you believe that your behavior doesn't predict results and that rewards in life aren't within your control. Having an external locus of control means that you attribute your successes or failures to outside factors.

What do you think happens to you if you think that your wins and successes are due to an outside force—luck, your team members, whatever—but not your own abilities? You doubt your own abilities and never learn that you're responsible for your successes. This can cause you to fear failure and make you feel like you can't achieve success on your own.

Moreover, what do you think happens to you if you attribute your *failures* to external forces? Two results can occur, one good and one not so good. The positive result is that you protect yourself from the frustration and self-blame that can occur when you hold yourself entirely responsible for work failures. You can prevent yourself from getting caught up in negative emotions when you don't achieve a desired result at work, and enable yourself to look at situations more objectively and understand how factors beyond your control (market pressures, the weather, your competitors, etc.) contributed to the failure.

The negative result? Only looking at external contingencies can give you a false sense of security about your own skills. When you only look at the outside factors that contributed to the failure, you neglect the opportunity to discover ways to improve yourself and grow in your career.

Internal Locus of Control

If you have an internal locus of control, you believe that your own actions and abilities directly lead to results. What do you think happens to you if you believe internal factors are responsible for your wins and successes? You begin to feel like you can create success yourself. This is a good thing! This is one of the ways to overcome the fear of failure. I'll tell you more about this later on.

However, what do you think happens to you if you believe internal factors are responsible for all of your problems and failures? You may become highly fearful of failure because you think the propensity to fail is strong within you. You can feel like you're a magnet for workplace debacles. Research suggests that people who have a stable internal locus of control regarding failures are more likely to be depressed (Costello 1982).

Perfectionism Rears Its Head

Personality traits and compulsive tendencies like perfectionism contribute to a fear of failure. The feeling that things need to be perfect or else they're awful is a polarized thinking pattern that is common with anxiety; it can quickly lead to a fear of failure.

In fact, many perfectionists are highly concerned about the possibility of failure. Perfectionists often also have a definition of failure that is quite severe: failure is anything less than perfect. This definition makes perceived failure extremely likely, right? Of course you'll be nervous! (Notice that I wrote "perceived failure"—this "failure" would probably be a success or a neutral event in the eyes of most people.)

You've Kept the Ball in Motion

The majority of behavior generally develops as a result of reinforcement: when you do something and it leads to a reward or positive outcome, you do it more. For example, if your perfectionist actions lead to favorable results—such as eliminating anxiety, creating a phenomenal memo, or giving an incredible presentation—you'll then engage in more perfectionist behaviors.

If you have a fear of failure at work, most likely you've done things—probably unintentionally—that have reinforced this fear. Having touched on perfectionism (see chapter 3 for a longer discussion of the relationship between perfectionism and anxiety), we'll now explore some other examples of fear-perpetuating behaviors.

Selective Attention

Let's say that you're someone who is highly nervous about the possibility of not succeeding in your career. You frequently worry about whether your actions will lead to a negative outcome. You doubt yourself and your decisions, thinking that you could easily make the wrong decision and plunge yourself down the slippery slope of *failure.*

If you're really concerned about all of these negative possibilities, what do you think you pay attention to? All of these negative possibilities! You focus on the problems that could make your fears come true. Because you're so nervous about how a failure—or even the tiniest difficulty—might bring you to the place that you don't want to be, you focus on all of your problems and perceived failures.

And what do you think happens when you focus on your problems and perceived failures? You just may make your fears come true.

Unrealistic Expectations

When your expectations are unrealistic, you set yourself up for failure. People who are nervous about failing at work often have at least one of two types of unrealistic expectations: an expectation of predictability or an expectation of control.

Predictability

Typically, those who fear failure would like to have a predictable future. A future without failure, right? And if you seek out predictability, what do you typically avoid? Risk. But if you want to meet your true capabilities, what do you usually need to do? Take some risks. See a pattern here?

First, there's often a trade-off between predictability and true success. Think of investing: When you invest in safer funds or bonds, you often sacrifice a high return. But what if what you're seeking is quick, short-term financial success? You may defeat your own goals by going after predictability and sacrificing risk. You may not "fail" per se, but if you're not meeting your true goals, you're not succeeding.

Second, you shoot yourself in the foot when you go after the promise of something that can't be promised. We all know how unpredictable jobs are in today's market. When you attempt to ensure career predictability, you attempt to attain the unattainable. It makes you nervous and takes you away from achieving your career satisfaction and profitability.

Control

The second unrealistic expectation is that you will be able to control your career. Unfortunately, we often attempt to control that which is not controllable.

Control is closely connected with anxiety. This is because when you try to control that which you actually have little control over, you become anxious. (Incidentally, trying to control anxiety itself can make you even more anxious. Sometimes the best thing to do is to *accept* the anxiety and keep forging ahead in your work in spite of it.)

If your goal is to control your career so you never experience failure, you've set a goal that is not only unrealistic, but actually sets you up for failure.

coaching point

Make a list of all of the things in your career that you feel you need to control in order to keep failure at bay. Once you've made your list, go through it item by item and think about how much you can actually control each item and how much your control is an illusion. What is trying to control these things costing you?

Joel's Story: A Self-Fulfilling Prophecy

Before Joel and I began to work together, he was trapped by his fear of failure. His fear came in large part from his overly critical parents. Growing up, if he got 90 percent on a test, he'd be asked what happened to the other 10 percent. His parents drew a lot of attention to his failures. Joel said they did this because it is what their parents had done and they honestly thought it would help him to excel. And in some ways it did—he set high standards for himself—but his fear of failure came at a cost.

Joel gave everything all he had because he was afraid what would happen if he didn't. He was a top athlete in college and president of several clubs and very active in his fraternity. It's pretty hard to give 100 percent to 100 different things! Because Joel was an "all-star" in so many areas, people expected great things from him. It was a good feeling, but it put a lot of pressure on him. Joel was very concerned about letting both himself and others down. Joel told me once that sometimes he felt like he was in a play, acting—and that soon the curtain would fall and his success would be over.

This pattern followed Joel into his first job in the financial industry. Joel told me, "It's funny because I was so afraid of failing, but in reality, I never really failed at much . . . until I began my job in an extremely competitive industry!"

There was no longer time to give everything 100 percent. Joel didn't know how to prioritize and he began falling behind. Joel became so nervous about not being outstanding that he grew increasingly tense and stressed. Although he wanted to enjoy his job and his friends at work, he couldn't.

Because of anxiety and self-imposed pressure at work, Joel's greatest strength became his greatest weakness. He was so convinced that he might let himself and other people down that he ended up crippling his own abilities. When you focus on something and frequently imagine that it will come true, it often does. This is true for many things in life. For example, if you're worried about a meeting at work, the night before you might think to yourself, "I'm never going to sleep tonight. It's going to be horrible, I'll be up all night worrying. And I'm going to be exhausted tomorrow since I won't get any sleep." What do you think—will you get a good night's sleep after having these thoughts? Probably not. Your thoughts shape your reality. Thinking "I will fail," or "I could fail," or "I'd better do such and such or I will fail" only increases the likelihood of failure.

Fear of Success vs. Fear of Failure

Believe it or not, many people actually fear *success*, not failure. This may sound crazy—after all, most people crave success—but often, even with changes that we really want, there are still trade-offs.

Fear of Success Quiz

Here's a brief quiz to determine if you fear success. Answer yes, no, or sometimes.

1. Do you fear that once you've attained your goals, you won't be able to sustain them? NO
2. Do you worry that once you've found success, you'll have nothing to motivate you? NO
3. Do you have thoughts like, "The fall from the top is a much harder fall"? SOMETIMES
4. Are you nervous about how others might view you once you've made it? (For example, do you worry that they'll view you as undeserving, arrogant, different, or snobby?) NO
5. Do you worry about problems that could occur when you earn more money? (For example, do you worry about having to pay more taxes, needing to make more decisions, or being asked for loans?) SOMETIMES
6. Are you concerned about having to manage or lead others? NO
7. Do you fear that success is a fragile achievement that could be destroyed at any time? YES
8. Do you wonder if you really deserve to be truly successful? NO

If most of your answers were either yes or sometimes, you may fear success as well as failure.

Do you notice anything about these fears about success? They're actually quite similar to fears about failure. It isn't really the success you fear, it's the negative consequences that could develop from the success—you fear success because it could lead to failure. The way to overcome your fear of success is actually the same as the way to overcome your fear of failure.

Overcoming the Fear of Failure

If you're serious about overcoming your fear of failure, you'll have to make some changes in your behavior and your thoughts. Keep in mind, however, that a certain level of fear is normal and can even be beneficial. Having some fear about changes and challenges shows that you understand that the stakes are high and helps you create a realistic estimation of risk so that you can choose your actions thoughtfully. The problems only come when fear paralyzes you, holds you back, or makes you anxious.

Changing Expectations

As you now know, when you expect failure, you increase your likelihood of failure. To combat this, you want to both reduce your nervousness and increase your confidence at work. One way to do this is to change your expectations.

What's So Bad About Failing?

Think about this question. Really—what's so horrible about failing? Have you ever found that something you thought was a disastrous failure ended up with a positive outcome? Ever have an experience in which you thought the consequence would be worse than it actually was?

It's helpful to think of failure as a continuum of negative consequences. Not every little failure leads to something catastrophic; there's a broad range of potential results that might occur.

In fact, some failures may even lead to significant successes. I'm sure you're familiar with stories about businesses going down horrible roads of failure before they suddenly turn around. It's sometimes in a failure that the biggest lesson is learned. In looking at your past mistakes, you may discover a million-dollar idea.

Moving On

Recovering from failure is also extremely important. The key to recovery is to learn whatever lesson can be learned from the experience and then move on; move toward activities that are directly in line with your career goals. If you get bogged down in defeat, you continue the process of being defeated. Instead, let your failures motivate you to try harder and go after what you really want.

The ability to forget and get over mistakes is one that is developed over time. You do need to work on it to make it happen. Often, as you're developing this ability, you'll have to consciously tell yourself to let your mistake go—and then get yourself busy with other aspects of your job that need to be attended to. As William Durant, founder of General Motors, put it, "Forget past mistakes. Forget failures. Forget everything except what you're going to do now and do it."

Predicting Success

By now, you know that if you predict failure, you're likely to attract failure—and that if you predict success, you're likely to attract success. So how do you predict success?

The first step is to pay attention to the successes you've already achieved. This may feel like a chicken/egg scenario. Certainly, this approach requires some confidence to do, but it's also the best way to build confidence. If you aren't yet confident, then try to look at your situation as an outside observer would. Work hard to view your career objectively.

Distancing yourself and being more objective can also help reduce the emotional reactions which may be your natural default.

Emotional reactions are more likely to impel you to predict failure. This is why it's helpful to gain a rational perspective.

coaching point

Make a list of your predictions for failure. Recognize these thoughts as they come into your mind. Write them down. Then transform them into predictions for success. Notice what happens. Do you find yourself thinking, "That will never happen," or is it exciting and inspirational? If a prediction for success seems too huge of a leap, break it down into smaller chunks.

Changing Locus of Control

Two different types of locus-of-control issues can lead to self-defeating thinking: a purely external explanation for successes and a primarily internal explanation for failures.

To transform your external explanations of success, begin to look for internal reasons for your successes. Catch yourself when you explain away a success as due to a source outside of yourself. Realize what *you* did to make it happen. Even if someone else in your office is primarily responsible for the success of your team's project, what role did you have? Even a backseat role counts. Everything adds up to create positive results. Recognize your contributions.

To deal with your internal explanations of failure, begin taking a look at the bigger picture. Remember that anxiety results when you scrutinize yourself heavily. A broader perspective can help both alleviate anxiety and reduce predictions of failure. Of course, it's important to maintain a healthy balance: you shouldn't be attributing every problem to someone or something else. But recognize that you aren't responsible for all of the problems that your office or business faces.

coaching points

1. When you start to dwell on failure after a difficult situation at work, brainstorm all of the factors that were beyond your control that may have contributed to the situation. Write these down in your notebook. Then write down any internal contributing factors. For each of the internal factors, write down several action steps that you can do to improve your skills and confidence.
2. Keep a success journal and write down all the ways that *you* created success for yourself.

Go for It!

The message of this chapter can be boiled down to a few short sentences (don't worry, you didn't waste your time reading the rest of it!): *The best way to overcome a fear of failure is to allow yourself to fail.* Take on some reasonable, calculated risks. Realize that it takes courage to do so and your confidence will build *regardless of the result*. Success is a journey, not the destination. As Jack Lemmon so aptly put it, "Failure seldom stops you. What stops you is the fear of failure."

Now that you aren't afraid to fail, you're ready to take on a new challenge: eliminating the crutches and self-limiting behaviors that you think help you—but don't. Ready? Read on!

CHAPTER 7

The Behaviors You Think Help—But Don't

> Tension is who you think you should be.
> Relaxation is who you are.
>
> —CHINESE PROVERB

What Do You Do to Help Yourself?

I have some bad news for you. You may have already figured it out: many of the things that you do to try to reduce your anxiety at work are actually likely to increase it. Anxiety often works paradoxically: things that seem to make you feel less anxious actually make you feel *more* anxious. Similarly, things that seem to make you feel more anxious actually make you feel less anxious.

Have I lost you? Just keep reading, it's a little weird. Basically, allowing yourself to experience what makes you anxious in the short term will help you overcome anxiety in the long term. Likewise, behaviors that allow you to stave off anxiety in the short term are going to end up making you experience *more* anxiety in the long term.

Put this book down for a minute and take out your notebook. Write down all of the strategies you use to manage your work-related anxiety. What do you do to prepare for work, either the night before or in the morning before you head out? What do you do in the moment that you're actually experiencing discomfort at work? What do you do after a distressing experience? In the next section, we'll sort behaviors into those that help and those that hurt.

Behaviors That Help

In a nutshell, there are two types of behavior that help. The first is any behavior you do that helps you confront the situation that is making you nervous. For example, if you typically become uncomfortable when speaking in front of a group, a helpful behavior on your list might be something along the lines of, "I make myself speak up even though I don't want to." We'll talk more about how to strengthen this type of behavior throughout this chapter.

The second type of helpful behavior is anything you do that helps you decrease your stress level. An increase in stress can lead to an increase in anxiety because stress taxes your coping resources and makes it more difficult to confront anxiety. Stress also helps enable procrastination—which enables anxiety. When you're under a lot of stress, you're less likely to push yourself to deal with the anxiety. For example, if you face a speaking situation while stressed out, you're more likely to tell yourself, "I can't deal with it today, maybe next time." Thus, stress enables anxiety.

We discussed several strategies for stress management in chapter 2. These strategies will help you take nonessential activities off your plate, freeing up time for you to focus on your high-priority activities—as well as time for more enjoyable activities. Do some experimentation to help you plan your relaxing and enjoyable activities. Try different things to see what is truly most relaxing or enjoyable for you.

Behaviors That Hurt

There are also two types of behaviors that hurt. The first is any behavior that keeps anxiety around; these tend to be avoidance and procrastination behaviors. We'll discuss these in detail in the next chapter.

The second type of harmful behavior is slightly more subtle; these are overcompensating behaviors. It may seem on the surface that these behaviors manage your anxiety, but typically they do not. (We discussed compensating behaviors in regard to public speaking in chapter 5; here we explore them more broadly.)

Compensating behaviors—or "safety behaviors"—are things you do to try to reduce your anxiety or make it less obvious to others. Anxiety researcher David Clark (2001) believes that they're actually subtle avoidance strategies designed to make the situation more manageable or stop your fear from coming true.

For example, if you're nervous about giving a presentation in front of your team, you may overprepare. This overpreparation then fuels anxiety and makes you come across as stiff, unnatural, and overly rehearsed. So what happens? Your presentation doesn't go very well and you become twice as nervous the next time you have to present. Research has found that safety behaviors are one of the primary culprits in keeping your anxiety around (Huppert, Roth, and Foa 2003). Although these safety behaviors appear on the surface to be naturally adaptive behaviors, in reality, they almost always backfire and end up increasing anxiety in the long term.

The Perils of Overcompensating

One of the main problems with overcompensating is that you draw more attention to that which you are trying to reduce. Remember: your focus expands whatever you're focusing on. When you focus on something to push down your anxiety, your anxiety expands. When you focus on doing something to make your anxiety less noticeable, it becomes more noticeable.

For example, someone who spills food in his lap during a business lunch may laugh and attempt to joke about it. But which tends to be more noticeable—the spill or the scene he creates? Joking around and laughing are overcompensating behaviors in this situation; although they're intended to diffuse tension, they end up making things worse by drawing attention to what others might not have noticed otherwise.

Recognize When You're Doing It

One major difficulty with overcompensating behaviors is recognizing when you're practicing them. Because you may think that they're helpful, they may not be obvious.

Step One

The first step to identifying overcompensating behaviors is to learn to recognize your thought patterns. Overcompensating behaviors are typically responses to perceived threats. You start feeling uncomfortable so you try to do something to feel better. So how do you realize when you start to feel nervous? Recognize the anxious thoughts that go through your mind. Anxious thoughts may be related to feeling embarrassed, losing status or respect, performing poorly, limiting your potential for growth in your career, or losing income. Be aware of these types of thoughts because they serve like a yellow light: a caution to be on the lookout to stop and not engage in overcompensating behavior.

Step Two

The next step is to notice how you're feeling. Are you tense? Do you have a stomachache or headache? Are you shaking or trembling? Light-headed or faint? Is your heart racing? Do you feel breathless? All of these physical reactions are related to feeling distressed and threatened. These physical responses often trigger the behaviors that aren't really helpful.

Step Three

The third step is to spot the overcompensating behavior itself. When you're prepared, through understanding your thought patterns and physical symptoms, you'll be able to spot problem behaviors right away. For example, if you know that an overcompensating behavior for you is to try to hide behind a podium or chair because you feel uncomfortable about your midsection, you'll start to recognize the behavior even as you begin to hide.

There are two primary reasons that people engage in overcompensating behaviors. The first is to try to reduce anxiety. You may rehearse how you're going to say something in your mind before you say it to reassure yourself that it'll come across well. The reason this often backfires is due to how you focus your attention: when you're focused on the activity that you do to reduce anxiety, you become focused on yourself. When you're focused on yourself, you become self-conscious. When you're feeling self-conscious, you become anxious.

The second reason people engage in overcompensating behaviors is to either hide anxiety or come across better to others in general. However, often when you try to hide something you actually draw more attention to the thing you're trying to hide. Also, when you try to hide your anxiety or come across better, you draw your *own* attention back to yourself. And again, when your attention is on yourself, you're likely to feel a heightened sense of anxiety.

Common Types of Overcompensating Behaviors

Here are some of the common ways overcompensating behaviors come up. Use this discussion to stimulate thought about how you may be overcompensating or relying on safety behaviors. At the end of this section, try to think about anything you do that isn't discussed here.

Making Jokes and Laughing

You've probably heard of the term "nervous laughter." Smiling and laughing when you're uncomfortable can be a sign of anxiety. You may make jokes and laugh on purpose as a way to compensate for anxiety, or you may respond this way unconsciously. The general idea is that if you're being funny, people will notice the humor and not the embarrassing moment or anxiety.

As you may know from your own experience, these strategies often backfire. Nervous laughter looks like nervous laughter—typically it's not very funny. In fact, it often just makes you feel bad for the person using the overcompensating behavior.

It's a rare individual who is able to come up with a clever joke in a situation in which they're distressed. When you're nervous, it's difficult to think clearly and creatively. For this reason, most jokes driven by anxiety don't go over very well, but instead actually draw more attention to you and increase your discomfort.

coaching point

To drop this overcompensating behavior, you first have to recognize when you do it. Next time you have the urge to make a joke or laugh when you're nervous, surf the urge—ride out the anxiety while allowing the urge to rise and fall like a wave. Don't allow yourself to react. It will pass. When the anxiety and potentially embarrassing moment have passed and you want to tell a joke, go for it! Just don't joke out of anxiety or embarrassment.

Mental Rehearsal

Do you ever plan out what you're going to say in your head before you say it? Do you carefully consider how something is going to sound and how you want it to come across? Do you attempt to avoid saying something stupid, embarrassing, ignorant, or offensive by rehearsing it before you say it? Do you lose track of conversations or what the other person is saying because you're so focused on planning what you'll say next?

This is one of the most common overcompensating behaviors. We've all done it. For example, you need to introduce yourself in a meeting and because you're so busy thinking about how you'll introduce yourself, you don't hear any of the other introductions.

Like many of the overcompensating behaviors, mental rehearsal can be beneficial to a certain degree. Many businesspeople have an "elevator speech" or way that they introduce themselves to others. This can be useful because it ensures that you know how to present yourself or sell your services or products.

Mental rehearsal can, however, also have a downside. Have you ever heard anyone sell their products or introduce themselves in a way that sounded canned and artificial? These people instantly turn you off—they appear fake and insincere. A little rehearsal of a key sales speech or a performance can be helpful but too much is harmful.

coaching point

Next time you need to have a conversation with someone at work or speak up in a meeting, try this: speak completely spontaneously. Don't mentally plan what you're going to say. Instead, allow yourself to focus on what the other person—or persons—is saying and track the conversation. Let yourself become immersed in the conversation rather than in your own mind. What do you notice? How is it different from when you rehearse? Is your anxiety level different?

Speaking spontaneously and immersing yourself in the conversation are highly effective strategies because they take your focus off yourself, thereby reducing self-consciousness and allowing you to follow the conversation better. If you're busy planning what you're going to say while someone else is talking, you won't be able to listen to their point; as a result, your statement is likely to be much less relevant and appropriate than if you had listened and answered spontaneously.

Mental rehearsal is actually a strategy for peak performance that I use with my clients. Allowing yourself to envision success is an extremely useful way to improve performance, whether the performance in question be a speech, an athletic feat, or an artistic event. The key here is that you do it ahead of time and *not* in the moment of your performance or conversation. (We'll discuss how to use mental rehearsal effectively further in chapter 12.) The problems with mental rehearsal as an overcompensating behavior are that it takes you out of the moment, prevents you from gaining valuable information from an interaction, and increases your self-focused attention.

Overpreparation and Reviewing

Overpreparation is another common overcompensating behavior, particularly for perfectionists. You may overprepare reports before giving them to your boss. You may spend hours reviewing your projects. You may frustrate your team members because you need excessive preparation while they're ready to go. The rationale is that your work cannot be perfect until it is prepared and reviewed very thoroughly. We've discussed the downsides to perfectionist behaviors throughout the book; these include annoying coworkers, reducing efficiency, increasing anxiety, and missing out on other aspects of life.

Reviewing can also come up in the social context of your job. Do you ever find yourself mentally reviewing conversations or speaking engagements after you've finished them? Is this helpful? Typically it isn't. Mental reviewing is often critical or judgmental. When you first finish an anxiety-provoking situation, you're still revved up from the anxiety. This means that your thought processes are likely to be distorted by your emotions. Emotions can cloud your mind and reduce your ability to judge a situation realistically.

When, after a difficult situation, you judge yourself negatively, what do you think happens the next time you're in that situation? Your anxiety is greater and more intense! For this reason, mental reviewing after a worrisome situation isn't helpful. If you want to review the situation constructively, wait at least a day—by that point, you won't be wrapped up in your anxiety and you may be able to come up with some useful points for improvement.

coaching points

1. Pick an upcoming project at work and prepare for the same amount of time a colleague would prepare for it. Do not allow yourself to prepare—or review—any more than this set amount! See what happens. Does your project fail miserably because you didn't overprepare? What benefits resulted from preparing and reviewing less? What can you do with your extra free time? Write down all of the benefits and enjoyable activities that resulted from this experiment. Refer to this list next time you're tempted to overprepare.

2. Banish all mental reviewing that follows directly after your performance situations. Take yourself out for a treat to celebrate having survived, go to the gym, or do something else to keep yourself from getting mired in unhelpful mental reviewing. A couple of days later, take out your notebook and write down your thoughts about the situation. Brainstorm ways to get training or help yourself develop particular skills. If you find that any of the things you write are vague complaints or worries, tell yourself that they are just anxiety-fueled thoughts and let them go.

Drinking or Eating or Not

You may find that you purposefully choose to eat or drink to help calm your nerves in distressing situations. Or you may worry about consequences of eating or drinking in front of others. Basically, whenever you're overanalyzing or trying too hard, an overcompensating behavior is likely to be present.

Purposefully Eating or Drinking

Some of my clients have said that they try to eat or drink something whenever they're around coworkers in unstructured settings. They feel it gives them something to do. Eating or drinking allows you to be active—not just sit there unsure of what to do with your hands. The problem with this is that, as with the other overcompensating behaviors, you don't want to send the message to yourself that you can't handle anxiety without the crutch of having a snack or drink in your hand— you'll be stuck then if there's no food or drink around.

Another problem comes into play when you consume alcohol in order to relax around coworkers. You still have the issue of depending on something to help manage your anxiety, but you have the additional issue of not knowing exactly how you'll act once you have a few drinks in you. Yes, you might feel a bit more relaxed—but that could lead to saying inappropriate comments. Or you might become so intoxicated that you make a fool of yourself. This is a classic example of how a compensating strategy backfires.

Purposefully *Not* Eating or Drinking

The most common reason that people avoid eating or drinking around others is to eliminate the possibility of spilling or getting something stuck in their teeth. Some people only eat specific finger foods that won't get caught in their teeth. Another reason you might avoid eating or drinking is to prevent anyone from noticing trembling hands or awkward gestures.

In addition to missing out on a good meal, you'll find that this overcompensating behavior is only likely to draw more attention to you. People will wonder why you're the only one not eating or drinking. You'll feel like you are in the center of attention that you were trying to avoid—and you may be hungry or thirsty!

coaching point

When it comes to eating or drinking around coworkers, simply tell yourself that you'll do whatever everyone else is doing. Plan a time to have lunch with colleagues or go to happy hour with coworkers. If you're hungry, eat. If you're thirsty, drink. Just be honest and don't try to convince yourself that you're not hungry so you can get away with engaging in your overcompensating behavior. Focus on remaining mindful of what's going on around you; you'll soon forget about any awkwardness or concerns regarding food.

Talking Too Little or Too Much

Another very common overcompensating behavior is talking either too little or too much. If you're someone who talks too little, ask yourself why this is the case. Many people who are nervous around coworkers restrict their words because they figure that the less said, the less chance they have of saying something that will come back to haunt them later. As a result, they may answer questions very briefly or pass them off to someone else. For example, "Uh, yeah, but I think Jonathan was really the one most involved with that project . . ."

If you talk too much, it may be because you're worried that you won't say something of value. I remember having this experience when I wrote papers in college. If I didn't know the answer, I'd ramble on and on, hoping that I'd collect some points for the things I did say and that the professor would overlook all of the filler in between. Of course this strategy backfires. You lose esteem in the eyes of your colleagues. Being able to communicate your ideas clearly and succinctly is one of the keys to success at work; this overcompensating behavior can be decidedly detrimental to your professional reputation.

coaching point

The next time you're in a meeting, practice answering questions with accuracy. The quantity of your speech should be dictated by the amount you need to say to give a great answer, not by your anxiety.

Notice that your initial rush of anxiety quickly subsides—typically after you've been speaking for about thirty seconds. If you escape from anxiety by answering too briefly, you'll never experience that your anxiety actually decreases with time. However, don't ramble: you'll know that you aren't saying something valuable—and this will increase your anxiety. Answer the question thoroughly and on point and you'll find your anxiety subsides relatively quickly.

Hiding

As I mentioned at the beginning of this chapter, anxiety can manifest itself in tons of different overcompensating behaviors. One final example we'll explore is hiding. Some common ways you may hide to escape things that make you anxious include:

- Standing behind a lectern, computer, or desk
- Sitting rather than standing in order to conceal parts of your body

- Putting your hands in front of your face
- Avoiding making eye contact with people (this is like how kids put their hands over their face and think they're invisible—we have a propensity to feel that someone doesn't see us if we don't see them, but of course this isn't true)
- Concealing your hands—avoiding gesturing, holding something in your hands, jiggling something in your pocket, or clasping your hands together so people don't notice any trembling
- Wearing drab, baggy, or nondescript clothes to keep attention off you
- Wearing flashy, showy, designer clothes or jewelry to make people notice your clothes and not you
- For women, purposefully wearing makeup—or not wearing makeup—to keep people from noticing you or your flaws

Do any of these sound familiar? If so, you've just spotted an overcompensating behavior that's likely to backfire and increase your nervousness.

coaching point

Go through the bullet points above and ask yourself whether you ever engage in any of these behaviors. Once you've identified one as a possibility for you, do it. When you do it, observe whether it's truly effective or whether it in fact makes you feel more self-conscious. Then, do the same activity without the overcompensating behavior. Notice how you feel in the situation. Once you've dropped the behavior (and become used to not relying on it), how is your anxiety affected? The key is to practice the activity without the overcompensating behavior frequently and amply.

Overcome Overcompensating

Follow the points in this chapter and do the exercises and coaching points described and you'll be well on your way to putting an end to overcompensating behaviors. Try hard to be open and honest with yourself in recognizing unhelpful behaviors; remember: they may feel helpful on the surface. Because overcompensating behaviors often serve as crutches, you may feel you can't get through certain situations without them. I don't want you to feel like that! I want you to feel like you can get through any situation in which anxiety comes up without having to depend on behaviors that may both backfire and keep your anxiety around.

Remember that with anxiety, the strategies that help you feel better in the short term are often the very ones that maintain anxiety in the long term. Which brings us to the next chapter, where we'll discuss the number one behavior that keeps anxiety around over the long term: avoidance.

CHAPTER 8

Avoidance, Procrastination, and Anxiety

> We are what we repeatedly do. Excellence, then, is not an act, but a habit.
>
> —ARISTOTLE

Avoidance and Anxiety

Want to know a surefire way to stay anxious? Don't do the thing that makes you nervous! When you fail to face a fear, the fear grows. For example, if you put off meeting with your boss all day, by the end of the day it's much harder to do. If you put it off for a couple of days, it's harder still. If you continue to avoid it, after a week it will probably have turned into a huge, nerve-wracking event. Let's explore how avoidance and anxiety interact at work.

How It Works

Have you noticed that you feel better when you avoid doing something that makes you nervous? If you're working on a difficult report, you might turn off the computer or check your e-mail or do something else to escape from your feelings of discomfort. Unfortunately, the next time you work on your report, you become anxious all over again. So you do something else. Thus, a cycle begins.

This cycle is one of the main reasons that anxiety sticks around and often even increases over time. It begins because you initially feel better when you avoid or put off doing something that makes you uncomfortable. If you're feeling better, you may wonder, what's the problem? The problem is twofold: First, your procrastination or avoidance doesn't let you learn the valuable lesson that you can confront difficult situations and get through them. Second, your procrastination or avoidance is then reinforced by the fact that you feel better. This makes you even more likely to continue avoiding the anxiety-provoking task.

This type of behavioral conditioning is called *escape conditioning*: to make an aversive response (anxiety, irritation) go away, we choose to escape from the situation. Of course we initially feel better when we turn off the computer and turn on our favorite television show! The problem is that we escape from our negative feelings before we have the chance to get through them and potentially develop positive feelings in the situation. As a result, you not only get rewarded for the unhealthy avoidance, you also miss out on getting rewarded for completing the distressing activity—and learning that it might not have been as bad as you expected.

Another problem that avoidance can lead to is the development of unhelpful negative associations. When a specific activity—e.g., working on the computer—has been paired with a negative reaction such as anxiety, frustration, or annoyance, the next time we engage in that specific activity, we're that much more likely to experience the negative reaction as well. If you've ever been sick after eating a certain food, you probably remember feeling sick the next time you smelled that food (and possibly the next, and the next). The same process can happen with activities at work, making it more likely that you will avoid the activity the next time.

The Fuel for the Fire

As you can see by now, anxiety loves avoidance! The more you avoid, the more anxiety hangs around. This is like giving a child candy when she begs and throws a tantrum—it will only encourage these behaviors. The next time she wants candy, she'll beg and throw a tantrum again. The more she gets the candy she wants, the more she'll beg and scream.

Avoidance slips down that same slippery slope. Allowing yourself to escape from an uncomfortable work situation makes it much more likely that you'll avoid the situation the next time around, too. It will also lower your threshold for anxiety, making you even more susceptible to avoidance and procrastination.

The Ups and Downs of Procrastination

Procrastination works in the same way as avoidance (procrastination is, in fact, a form of avoidance). Likewise, procrastination often gets rewarded, but again, these rewards come at a cost.

The Rewards of Procrastination

If you're a procrastinator, you're probably this way simply because you've been able to get away with it without suffering any major negative consequences. Although you may have experienced intense pressure during the final hour before a project was due, in the end, things turned out okay—making you more likely to procrastinate the next time.

The other main reward of procrastination is the short-term reduction in anxiety that occurs when you tell yourself, "I won't deal with that now, I'll wait till later." As you know, the more you put something off, the more anxiety-provoking it can be when it's actually time to do it. Which brings us to the downside of procrastination.

The Downside of Procrastination

If you can get away with procrastinating and still accomplish everything you need to, what's the downside? Well, the biggest potential problem is that you may *not* always accomplish everything. Or maybe you didn't finish everything as well as you could have because you ran out of time or crumbled under the pressure. After you've put something off for a while, it becomes much harder to begin it. And by that point, there's usually a lot more pressure—because there's now much less time to complete the task.

While some time pressure can be helpful in stimulating motivation and improving performance, too much often leads to a decline in performance. When you do your work at the last minute, the resources necessary to improve the quality of your work may not be available to you. Most of your colleagues won't be available at midnight on a Sunday in the same way that they would have been at midday on a Monday when your project was first assigned.

Another difficulty with procrastination is that typically you aren't calm or anxiety-free while you're putting the project off. Unless you're great at denial, the project most likely feels like a monkey on your back, weighing you down until you finally get around to taking care of it.

Sal's Story: Work Without Deadlines

One of my clients, Sal, a self-described procrastinator, used to be a high-powered executive with a Fortune 500 company. His procrastination caused him some serious problems in corporate America. The main problem was the annoyance and inconvenience he caused his colleagues by taking longer to complete his projects. But overall, Sal met his deadlines and his work was excellent—so good that he quickly moved up in his company and was able to retire in his late forties.

At this point, Sal decided to open his own business. He'd always dreamed of being an entrepreneur and now he finally had the financial resources and time to be one. But there was a problem brewing: Sal's procrastination.

When you're the boss of your own company, you set the deadlines. There was now no one to tell Sal when things needed to be completed. What do you think happened? He procrastinated. He became increasingly anxious and his company lost profitability.

Procrastination and Perfectionism

As you can imagine, these two are not a good combination. Some perfectionists put things off until they feel that they can dedicate themselves to the task at hand and do it perfectly. This can mean waiting a very long time, because there is rarely—if ever—a perfect time to devote yourself completely to your work.

Imagine what happens if you procrastinate and then have only limited time available to complete your activity—but still have a compelling urge to do it perfectly! This is definitely a recipe for intense anxiety. To overcome this deadly mix, something needs to give, either perfectionism or procrastination—or better yet, both!

Second-Guessing Yourself

Do you have a tendency to second-guess yourself? Do you often wonder whether you've made the correct decision? Do you feel the need to ask someone? Is it hard for you to make the decision in the first place? Do you feel like you second-guess your instincts and end up researching and collecting a lot of information before settling on a decision?

These are all characteristics of second-guessing; I see them as subtle strategies of avoidance. If you spend a lot of time asking people for their opinions, or go over and over a decision in your mind, you're putting off making the decision. If you second-guess a decision you've already made, you're avoiding dealing with the implications of the decision, good or bad.

One of the worst parts about second-guessing is that it undermines your confidence. Imagine that your boss second-guessed everything you did. You'd assume that he had no confidence in you, right? The same holds true for yourself: your second-guessing of yourself causes you to lose confidence in yourself.

Second-guessing can also waste valuable time. When you have a job that requires the ability to be decisive and take action quickly, there's no room for second-guessing; second-guessing could cost you your reputation, your performance, your safety, or your job.

The Solutions

Without procrastinating, let's jump right into solutions for overcoming avoidance, procrastination, and second-guessing.

Avoid Avoiding

There's a simple solution to the problem of anxiety-provoking avoidance: always confront the things that make you anxious and stay with them until your negative reaction subsides. While this is often easier said than done, it's worth doing because it's extremely effective in reducing avoidance.

First, confront that which makes you anxious rather than avoid it. (It's best to do this multiple times: things get easier as we get used to them.) Second, do that which makes you anxious for an extended period of time, until your anxiety subsides. If you do it quickly and then escape, you'll only learn to avoid anxiety. If you stick with it, you'll find that you actually become less anxious over time. Additionally, your confidence will increase as you get results that you can feel good about; and your avoidance and procrastination will start to decrease. (The cycle works both ways.)

The key to success with this approach is that you *keep doing the activity that you wanted to avoid until a positive result occurs.* For example, if you're working on a business project, the positive result could be that you begin to write down some great ideas, that you come up with the initial stages of an outline, or that your frustration or negative feelings start to decrease.

Everyone asks me how long it will take to habituate to anxiety and begin to feel better. Unfortunately, there's no single answer to this question: it depends on the intensity of the anxiety, the nature of the situation, and your own biological makeup. We know that the human body naturally habituates to anxiety within somewhere between a few minutes and ninety minutes. After the initial adrenaline rush (from the activation of the sympathetic nervous system), the parasympathetic nervous system kicks in and produces a more relaxed feeling.

Remember to stick with your work for a while so you don't fall into the trap of escape conditioning and end up wanting to escape again the next time. If you keep approaching a difficult situation, you'll find that it takes less time to calm down from the anxiety the situation provokes. If you remember nothing else from this book, remember this: *avoid avoiding.*

Time Management

One of the best ways to keep yourself from procrastinating is to simply not let procrastination begin. Procrastination is like a burglar trying to get into your house: if the front door isn't open, he'll try the back door—and if that isn't open he'll try the windows. Similarly, when you procrastinate you tell yourself something like, "I'll just catch up with some coworkers for a few minutes." If that doesn't work to get your mind off what you need to do, you might then tell yourself, "I should really check my e-mail." Effective time management is like the security system or Rottweiler that protects your home from a burglar: it doesn't allow room for procrastination to sneak in.

Creating Structure

As much as we may rebel against and resist making a structure for ourselves, structure prevents procrastination. After working with top executives, business owners, and community leaders, it has become clear to me that the people who manage their time well are the people who structure it and schedule it. Of course you need to build in some flexibility to handle various issues that come up—but overall, your days should be structured.

If you have an assistant or administrator, your time may be already scheduled for you. Although this can help you keep to a schedule, there is a risk that you may become dependent on your assistant. This is risky because your assistant may not always be there—or you may want to go into a field that requires you to independently create your own schedule, as my client Sal from the case study above did.

If you create your own schedule, get into the habit of making a schedule for a week or a month and then updating it every morning or evening. You can use technology to help you—synchronize a pocket PC with your desktop or laptop; create reminders that pop up and tell you what you're supposed to be working on.

If you can't afford—or don't have, or don't like—such technology, a good old-fashioned pad or paper calendar will work just fine. However, don't just write everything down on a to-do list—it's likely to just become long and intimidating. Instead, make a one-page list of tasks that need to be completed and then file those tasks into specific time slots in your day.

A good red flag for problems with creating structure is any thought that begins with "I'm just going to wait for . . ." Don't wait for anything. Put it into your schedule and then stick to your schedule.

Prioritizing and Goal Setting

We've talked a lot about how prioritizing is important to overcoming anxiety and perfectionism. Prioritizing is also important in helping you achieve success in your career and happiness in your life. Once you've prioritized your goals, you can then create goals that are achievable and motivating.

It's a big mistake to have no formulated career goals—or to have only vague goals. Trying to work toward an undefined goal is like driving at night with no lights on your car: you can't know where you're going. You have to know what your goal is to achieve it. As Thoreau wisely said, "In the long run, we only hit what we aim at."

Goal-setting theory tells us that it's not only important that you set goals, but that *how* you set goals is also critical. You may have heard of SMART goals, created by an unknown marketing and motivational genius. It's a concept designed to help you develop inspiring, achievable goals. Creating and sticking to SMART goals can truly change your life, especially if you haven't really been setting specific goals up until now.

A *SMART goal* is one that is: Specific, Measurable, Action-focused, Realistic, and Time-limited. You can easily see how these types of goals can greatly help you structure and use your time—they have a time component built right in. For a goal to be SMART, you must know what exactly it is that you want to do (specific) and how you will know when it is done (measurable). The goal must also be both behavioral (action-focused) and something that you can actually do (realistic). And finally, there must be a specific deadline for the goal's completion (time-limited)

An example of good SMART goals for a journalist might be: By Wednesday, research my magazine article by interviewing three experts. By Thursday, read five articles and scan two books on the topic. By 5 P.M. on Friday, complete the outline of my article.

A Reward System

One of the best ways to get and stick to a schedule is to give yourself positive reinforcement. If you have children, you've probably tried this strategy with them—maybe with a "Once you finish your peas, you can watch TV," or a "Once your bedroom is clean, you can play a video game." Although we all know this strategy works, we often fail to employ it.

This strategy is the opposite of procrastination. When you procrastinate, you say, "I'll just watch one TV show and then I'll finish up my research." This takes away the powerful reinforcing reward of your favorite TV show and makes it that much less likely that you'll accomplish your task. When you use a reward system, you give yourself a time limit to accomplish your task—which both puts a healthy degree of pressure on you (since it's not last minute) and gives you added incentive to accomplish your task.

Climb the Ladder

It can be difficult to go from avoiding something altogether to doing it 100 percent. If it's too hard for you to just plunge headfirst into a goal or work project, create a series of steps—a ladder—to help you.

Let me caution you about using this procedure. Have you ever tried to get into a cold pool by putting one foot in, then getting out; putting your other foot in, then getting out; putting your leg up to your knee in, then . . . ? Do you see where I'm going with this? Two problems can occur.

First, the whole process can take a long time—and you can wind up procrastinating, which is exactly what you're trying to avoid. Second, with this strategy, you may never actually get into the pool—because you got too cold, ran out of time, got bored, etc.

coaching points

Try these exercises to create and stick to a schedule:

1. Using a planner, make a schedule for your week. Here's a helpful hint: schedule short blocks of time for errands and catch-ups as well as your regular duties. Have a list of errands and catch-ups ready every evening or morning and file specific activities into the blocks of time you've reserved. (Using computer software for this process is great: you can just cut and paste.) You can remove a task when it's done, but if you don't finish it, it must go back onto your list (which can be very frustrating; sometimes even frustrating enough that it will give you extra incentive to get it done).
2. Write down your SMART goals. Be sure to include goals related to your career performance and advancement. Each week, check your progress on these goals; be sure you've included specific action steps on your calendar to help you meet these goals.
3. In your notebook, make a list of small and large rewards for yourself. A small reward might be watching your favorite TV show, walking the dog in the park, having a drink with friends, or going to a cycling class at the gym. Small rewards are the types of things you can do after you've completed all of your scheduled activities. Large rewards are the things you'll do for yourself after you've completed your SMART goals. A large reward might be a weekend skiing, a new outfit from a favorite designer, or a day of golf at a top golf course.

The key to using the ladder system is to push yourself along quickly. Recognize that if you take too long on any one step, you may not get to the next step. Remember: the whole point of the steps is to get you into the pool—or to the top of your list of goals. Going through the motions in a series of steps can, however, be very helpful; with each step you accomplish, you gain momentum and motivation for tackling future steps.

coaching point

In your notebook, draw a ladder or a series of steps. Put your ultimate feared or avoided activity at the top. This is the thing that is so important to do but that you absolutely don't want to do. At each rung on the ladder, or under each step, write one action step that will help you reach your goal. These action steps don't necessarily need to be directly related to one another; they can be different activities that you avoid.

For example, for a salesperson, the top of the ladder might be to make a cold call to a prospect in front of her boss. One step on her ladder might then be to make a follow-up call in front of colleagues. Another step might be to write a letter and follow up with a call in private. Another step might be to give a product demonstration in front of an existing client. Once you have your steps written down (a maximum of ten), put them in order, beginning with the least anxiety-producing activity as the first step all the way to the most anxiety-producing activity as the final step.

Trust Your Intuition

If you're plagued by second-guessing yourself, you need to learn to trust your intuition. Second-guessing yourself involves doubting your intuition or natural inclination. The best way to learn to trust your intuition is to follow two simple steps: first, begin to listen to it; second, begin to act on it. The more you get used to hearing your intuition, the more you'll listen to it and feel confident about acting on it—and as you act on it, you'll also learn how often it's actually right on target.

Another important step in learning to trust your intuition is to recognize how to best rely on others. People who second-guess themselves often ask for reassurance or opinions from others. Although this is useful in some circumstances, it can also keep you from listening to, and acting on, your intuition—and keep you from developing confidence in the fact that you can make a sound judgment independently, thereby making you more likely to ask people the next time you need to make a decision, too.

The opposite extreme is someone who doubts himself, but feels that he *should* be able to make the decision on his own, and thus never asks for help. This is equally problematic: it keeps you from learning from others. One way we develop our knowledge and confidence is in learning from others; if you prevent yourself from doing this, your own abilities won't grow to their fullest.

coaching points

1. Develop your awareness of your intuition by listening for it. Often, to hear your intuition you need to first calm the mental chatter and noise that masks it. Many people find activities like daily meditation, yoga, walks in nature, quiet time in a warm bath, or listening to jazz or classical music helpful in quieting the mind.
2. Once you have an instinct or inclination, try it out. See that your instincts are often right on. Even if an inclination didn't produce the desired result, ask yourself what you can learn from it. Is it still a good thing that you acted on it? It's usually worse to think, "I had a feeling this is how it would go—I should have listened!" than to think, "I followed my gut instincts, but things didn't work out this time."
3. If you're someone who asks for a lot of reassurance, try to cut down on your soliciting of opinions from others for a while. See whether you can handle things just as well (or better!) on your own.
4. If you're someone who rarely asks for input from others, try to ask more questions; educate yourself. It can be very useful to see how others' responses are the same as your inclinations. This process both validates your intuition and helps build confidence. When others' responses differ from your inclinations, you can learn from them—even if you still decide to stick with your original inclination.

CHAPTER 9

The Nervousness That Flares Around Others

"Alone we can do so little; together we can do so much."

—HELEN KELLER

The Fear of Being Judged

Do you ever feel uncomfortable, tense, or shy around your coworkers, colleagues, or boss? Even if you're not paralyzed with fear, you may still feel ill at ease around others. You may feel that you need to be constantly "on," or always pay attention to how you're coming across. When you walk out of the office in the evening, or when you finally get some time to yourself, you may breathe a sigh of relief.

If this sounds like you, your workplace anxiety is connected to being around others. For some, this anxiety is greater if the other in question is:

- A boss or someone who evaluates your work performance
- Senior to you in the company
- Someone to whom you need to sell or promote your work/products
- Someone you view as more intelligent, skilled, or highly regarded than yourself

In addition, many find that the number of others around them makes a difference. For example, it may feel worse to you when it's just you and someone else, because all of their attention is then focused on you. On the other hand, it may feel worse to you when there are many people around, because then there are lots of people you might embarrass yourself in front of.

Worrying That Others Are Judgmental

The most typical concern related to being uncomfortable around others at work is a concern that people might judge you negatively. You may feel that others will scrutinize your actions, appearance, nonverbal behavior, or statements.

Now, depending on your workplace and your coworkers, this will be more or less true. Remember: anxiety magnifies emotional reasoning. Thus, even if there is only a single grain of truth behind your concern, your nervousness may amplify it dramatically. If, in your office, there's someone who is judgmental, your anxiety may make you feel like you have *many* overly critical coworkers. Similarly, if your workplace has high standards and expectations, your anxiety may make you feel that anything short of a 100 percent performance at all times will be viewed as completely unacceptable.

Of course, some environments are more judgmental—particularly about certain aspects—than others. For example, if you're working in the modeling industry, you may feel a high degree of anxiety about looking thin and attractive. This anxiety is likely to be founded on a legitimate degree of pressure—many people who work in the modeling industry (and not just the models) say that people look at you and judge your appearance regularly. Most other fields, however, aren't so appearance-focused.

It's important to consider how realistic your perceptions of the judgments of others really are. You're probably tempted to describe your perceptions as very realistic, but keep in mind that a high-pressure, fast-paced work environment isn't synonymous with one in which people are always critically judging and negatively evaluating one another.

Most people simply aren't in the habit of paying much attention to the behavior of others. And even when you do capture the attention of your colleagues, it's unlikely that they're going to be judgmental.

coaching point

Make a list of all of the situations in which you've felt that others were looking at you, being critical of you, or judging you. Include any situation that has come up over the past month or so in which you felt nervous or uncomfortable around people that are associated with your job. We'll revisit this list in the next coaching point.

Being Judgmental Yourself

In working with hundreds of clients, I've found that some of the people who worry most about being judged negatively are actually on the critical side themselves. These individuals tend to hold high standards for themselves—and sometimes for other people as well.

The first scenario includes people who are either perfectionists or very self-critical. (If chapter 4 was particularly relevant to you, you may fall into this camp.) Because you view yourself critically, you naturally assume that others do the same. And even while you may rationally know that you're your own worst enemy, it may still feel like others are looking at you critically.

The second scenario includes those who scrutinize others. It takes an open, honest appraisal of yourself to recognize or admit that you do this. I've seen this critical scrutiny come up in mainly two ways: First, in being critical of others' speech and actions. For example, you may feel the need to correct a typo on a memo someone sent out. Or it may drive you nuts when someone mispronounces a word. Or you may find yourself looking at someone's outfit and wondering why in the world he thinks his tie and shirt match. More generally, you may often find yourself thinking that people are incompetent or don't deserve to be in their positions. You may be a perfectionist, or you may be someone who is highly attentive to detail and intolerant of mistakes—or you may be both.

If this is the way you think about others, then it makes sense to think that others think this way about you. We tend to make the assumption that others think as we do. Of course you'll feel judged by others if you're someone who often judges others!

The second way I've seen this scrutiny of others come up is in overly comparing yourself to others. Some ways that people commonly compare themselves to others—not necessarily in a judgmental way—include:

- Social status
- Appearance
- Intelligence
- Work level

- Years with the company
- Number of reports or subordinates
- Responsibilities
- Family life
- Status symbols (e.g., cars and jewelry)
- Ability to present ideas well
- Age (or appearance of age)

If you look to see how people are better than you, of course you'll then find some ways that people *are* (at least in your view) better than you. This will only make you more nervous or depressed—and may cause you to then compare yourself with even more people.

One result of social comparison—a result that many people feel uncomfortable with—is our interest in seeing other people fail. Have you ever read about a celebrity breakup and felt a little happy about it? If so, this is totally normal. This is linked to the human need to feel like part of the pack. It's uncomfortable to feel like others are better off than us; when something appears too good to be true (like the marriage of two gorgeous, rich, famous people) part of us wants it to be proved too good to be true.

Feeling this way doesn't make you a bad person. However, any natural tendency can become negative if taken to an extreme. If you're constantly walking around looking at others and hoping they fail miserably in all of their endeavors, you'll want to work on your attitude.

More likely, you probably just observe the actions and appearance of others to see how you compare. When someone isn't completely secure in himself or herself (and who is?), they're more prone to observe those around them carefully. Because of this, you may have a heightened awareness of your coworkers.

This heightened awareness can then affect your anxiety level by causing you to become caught up in self-focused attention. Remember how self-focused attention affects you? It makes you more self-conscious. You may wonder how a heightened awareness of others translates into self-focused attention. This is because when you're making social comparisons, you're not merely observing others and moving on, you're turning these observations back upon yourself. For example, your thoughts might go something like this: "Wow, Jennifer is an extremely confident speaker. Even speaking she looks relaxed and calm, while I'm sitting here next to her feeling tense because I may need to speak, too. I'm just sitting here and I'm looking more nervous and stressed than Jennifer and she's the one presenting. That must look weird. I wish I were more confident like Jennifer . . ."

See how it comes back to the self-focus? If you were just noticing things in your environment (your coworkers being one of those things), you probably wouldn't be anxious. In fact, this kind of external focus cures some forms of anxiety. But when you're bringing your observations negatively back to yourself, it's only likely to increase your anxiety.

coaching point

Use the list you made in the previous coaching point of situations in which you were nervous around coworkers to consider what types of judgments typically come up for you. Identify the specific types of judgments that you commonly make, paying particular attention to whether you judge others or yourself more harshly.

As you look over your statements, ask yourself: Do you frequently feel like you're being judged? If so, what aspects do you fear that people are judging you on? Also, are you critical of others? Do you compare yourself to others often? If so, what criticisms or comparisons arise?

Common Situations

Anxiety around others is very likely to occur in certain situations in the workplace. (You may find that some of these situations are on the list you worked on in the coaching points.) The following list of anxiety-producing situations is necessarily incomplete: nervousness around others can crop up any time you're around people, in or out of the workplace.

Interviews

Interviews are intimidating for many people—even for those who do not otherwise experience workplace anxiety. The higher the stakes, the more nerve-wracking the interview. If it's a job you really want, or a job that would afford you the opportunity to move to a city you'd love to live in, there'll be a lot of pressure riding on the interview.

Being Interviewed

The primary cause of nervousness around others at work is concern about being evaluated. Thus, interviews are likely to be high-anxiety situations—when you're being interviewed, you're by definition being evaluated.

Think about the last time you had an interview (if you have one coming up, think about that). What was—or is—your worry? Most likely, you're concerned that you won't answer questions well. You may worry that you'll say the wrong thing—or won't say the right thing—or won't have anything to say at all. You probably fear that your inability to nail interview questions will lead to your not getting the position, which could then hamper your career advancement.

Leading an Interview

Some people also feel uncomfortable about conducting interviews. This can be particularly true when you feel a candidate would be a tremendous asset to your organization.

For example, let's say that you own your own business and you've just found the ideal candidate to run your information technology department. You can clearly see how this person could help your business take off. He's flying in from the opposite coast to meet with you, but you know that he has several other job meetings and interviews lined up. You also know that you can't offer him the salary that some of your competitors can. As a result, you may feel nervous about conducting his interview, in part because you probably feel that you need to sell the job to him. (This is the same form of anxiety that comes up with sales meetings.)

New managers also sometimes feel uncomfortable with their new responsibilities. To effectively interview someone, you have to appear professional and knowledgeable while at the same time representing your company well. This can be nerve-wracking. We'll talk about this idea some more in the next chapter.

Entering a Meeting Late

You race out your door, knowing that you're barely going to have time to make it to work before your nine A.M. meeting with your department—including some of the senior-level executives. "I hope I don't hit any traffic!" you think to yourself. But before that thought can even finish going through your head, you have to slam on your brakes, blinded by all the red brake lights in front of you. "Oh no!" you think, "I'm going to have to walk into the meeting late and everyone will turn around and stare at me. The room will fall silent and all eyes will be on me as I make my way to my seat. No one's going to be interested in hearing excuses about traffic—my boss will think I'm not dedicated."

Does any of that sound familiar to you? When you enter a room after others are already seated, do you feel extremely conscious of all eyes being on you? Do you hate that moment of silence when everyone turns to see who it is that arrived late? Have you ever avoided going to a meeting because you're going to have to walk in late?

If so, you're not alone. This is something that many people feel uncomfortable with and often try to avoid. You might avoid getting to meetings late by purposefully leaving extremely early to ensure that you get there on time. Or you might skip a meeting altogether so you don't have to experience that feeling of walking in late. More subtly, you might avoid the situation by looking down and avoiding eye contact as you enter late.

Office Parties

When the holidays roll around, I always get requests from media outlets to talk about things like, "How to Survive Your Office Holiday Party," "How to Recover from a Blunder at Your Office Party," and "What to Do at the Holiday Party When You're Shy."

Clearly, office parties are difficult for many people!

Office parties can be particularly uncomfortable if you're either shy or anxious. While there is some correlation between shyness and social anxiety, some people are simply shy without begin nervous around others. These are the people who are comfortable being quiet, comfortable observing rather than participating. However, even if *you* feel comfortable, you may worry that others could negatively interpret your reticence.

Some people are actively uncomfortable about their shyness. If you feel this way, you may worry about how you are coming across to others and agonize about what to say. You may feel awkward just standing around while others are chatting and joking with each other.

One of the most difficult aspects of office parties is typically their lack of structure. People mill around mingling. There isn't much order as to where people sit or stand, or who you talk to. It can be especially uncomfortable if you walk in and people are already grouped together in conversations. You may then wonder if you should interrupt a group and join in, or just stand there and wait for someone to initiate a conversation with you.

The other main difficulty with office parties, happy hours, and get-togethers is that they typically call for you to interact with your coworkers in a different way. For some, the informality and casualness of an out-of-office event is relaxing and enjoyable. But for others, trying to relate to coworkers on a friendly, less formal level can feel strange and uncomfortable. The way that you react in these situations depends on both your personality and your concerns about interacting with others.

Watercooler Conversations

Watercooler conversations can present similar challenges. One potential difference, however, is that these casual conversations are in the midst of a workday. One minute you're wearing your "serious worker" hat while the next you're joking with colleagues about the reality show you watched the night before.

Another difference is that office happy hours or parties frequently entail the consumption of alcohol. Drinking alcohol may increase or decrease anxiety. (As we discussed in chapter 7, alcohol use can backfire—although you may drink to feel more comfortable and avoid doing something embarrassing, what's more likely to occur when you drink a lot of alcohol? Doing something embarrassing, of course.) Casual conversations at the office typically do not involve alcohol. This may make these interactions feel less comfortable to you. At a bar, everyone is relaxed and casual. Around the watercooler or in your coworker's office, the social setting is not so clear. It may feel like a situation that calls for casual interactions, but at the same time, you're still at work—it can be very confusing and discomfiting.

Concern About Inadvertent Sexual Harassment

Some of the male executives I've worked with express concern about unwittingly perpetuating sexual harassment in the workplace. (Sexual harassment can, of course, be perpetrated by either a man or a woman, but I've heard this concern voiced mainly by male executives, so I'm using their examples here.) Some men are afraid that in joking around with a male coworker, they'll say something that's offensive to a female coworker. Although they typically recognize what is clearly inappropriate to say, they may also worry, for example, about how a compliment to a female coworker like "you look nice today" might be interpreted.

I'm very happy about the greater sensitivity to sexual harassment in the workplace that has occurred over recent years. Like many good things, however, cautiousness taken to an extreme level can create anxiety. I advise my clients to be sensitive to what they say in the workplace and whom they say it to. If they have no history of saying offensive comments, then most likely they're being appropriately sensitive. If they do say something and worry that someone overheard it and was offended, I typically advise them to approach this coworker directly and apologize and assure her that it will not happen again.

Business Lunches

Business lunches can present a whole slew of potentially embarrassing moments. You could be sitting there smiling at your coworkers with a big piece of spinach wedged between your teeth. You could spill your can of Coke on the lap of the executive vice president. You could get bright red marinara sauce on your crisp white shirt. And these debacles don't even include what can happen when you open your mouth and say something!

A business lunch may be a casual lunch where you take a break from working or it may be a working lunch. Think about which type of lunch presents more anxiety for you. If the casual lunch is more anxiety-provoking, it may be that you're finding a lack of clarity about the lunch's goals difficult to deal with. With a working business lunch, it's always clear you're working on a specific project; casual lunches tend to have much less clear goals. Simply hanging out and chatting can feel uncomfortable.

Meeting Someone New

There's typically a lot of pressure involved in meeting a new work associate, prospect, boss, or employee—you want to make a good first impression. Everyone knows the expression "You never get a second chance to make a first impression." This puts a lot of pressure on us to make that great first impression.

In reality, even though it may be difficult, you can recover from a negative first impression. In social psychology there's something known as the *halo effect*. People form an impression of you and then see your other actions in line with that impression. If they form a positive or favorable perspective of you, you get a positive halo. Then your other actions (even if they are neutral or slightly negative) are viewed positively. If you make an unfavorable impression, you similarly get a negative halo.

When you meet someone new with whom you won't have a lot of contact, you have only a few opportunities to reformulate the impression you make. For this reason, the initial impression you make is more important with someone you won't see very often. If you see someone every day, you'll shape your professional relationship over time. After a few weeks or months, they may not even remember their first impression of you unless it was remarkably good or remarkably bad (e.g., you spilled your cup of hot coffee on their lap!).

Becoming Comfortable Around Others

Wouldn't it be wonderful to go into work and feel relaxed and at ease all day long? Wouldn't it be great to go to office get-togethers and meetings feeling confident and presenting yourself well? Don't you think you'd be more effective and successful at work if you weren't using valuable mental energy figuring out how others were evaluating you? Of course you would!

The thousand-dollar question is how to feel more comfortable around others at work. By this point in the book, you probably already have a few ideas of what you need to do differently. Let's go through steps you can take to increase your comfort and decrease your anxiety around others at work (these steps should sound familiar).

What's the Worst-Case Scenario?

At some point, when you've been worried about something, someone has probably asked you, "What's the worst thing that could happen?" This is actually a very important question in overcoming anxiety. As we've discussed, anxiety tends to blow things out of proportion. The key equation for anxiety is this:

Overestimation of Risk
+ = Anxiety
Underestimation of Ability to Cope

The worst-case scenario question helps you to get at the first variable, your overestimation of risk. When you really look at what you're afraid of, you may find that the worst thing that can happen isn't as horrible as you initially thought. The trick to using this question is that you really consider the worst possible outcome. Even if you're mostly aware that this outcome is unrealistic, the anxious part of your brain is probably still hanging onto it as something that *could* happen.

The best way to handle the worst possible outcome is to face it. It's like watching a frightening suspense movie. If you were to turn off the movie right as it began to get disturbing, you'd probably spend the rest of the night imagining all of the horrible and scary outcomes that could have occurred. Your mind would get very creative about the frightening endings. If, however, you were to watch the movie all the way through, your mind would probably just move onto other things afterwards. The movie might even be enjoyable and the ending might be great. When you confront your anxiety's worst possible situation, you're likely to realize both that it's unlikely and that it's less frightening than you initially thought.

How Might Someone Else See It?

Our imagination is usually a lot worse than the reality. When you face something, you're able to get used to it—as a result, you may realize either that it isn't really all that bad or that your worst fear really isn't realistic. And even if it is realistic, you should still ask yourself:

How Likely Is It?

Ask yourself how many times your feared outcome has previously come true. Let's say that you're worried that you'll act like a total idiot in front of your boss at the office holiday party—and that this will ultimately lead to your not being promoted and even eventually being fired. If, knowing yourself and your boss, you decide that this worst-case scenario is somewhat realistic, ask yourself how likely it is. Then calculate how many times you worried about it happening. If you've worried about it at every office social function over the past three years, and your office averages one event per month, you've had the worry thirty-six times. Now ask yourself how often has it come true. Again, do the math. You'll realize first, you've never truly made a fool of yourself; and second, you've never been fired. So, your worry has come true precisely zero out of thirty-six times. Therefore, based on past experience—and past experience is the best predictor available for future events—the realistic likelihood of your fear coming true is 0 percent.

These two questions—what's the worst-case scenario and how likely is it—address the first variable in the anxiety equation: your overestimation of the risk you face and the likelihood that the outcome you fear will come true. At this point, you should have a more realistic estimation of the risk. But *even if* the risk were to turn into reality . . .

Could You Handle It?

Now we're getting at the second variable in the anxiety equation: your underestimation of your ability to cope. Let's say that you actually did trip as you tried to sneak into a meeting late, thereby drawing all sorts of negative attention to yourself. Even though this is unlikely, how would you handle it?

Ask yourself how long the negative outcome is likely to last. Yes, your coworkers may think you're clumsy or people may make certain assumptions about your lateness. But how long are these thoughts likely to stay on their minds? Forever? More realistically, probably the duration of the meeting at most. Could you handle being embarrassed for forty-five minutes, or would that be the end of the world?

What are some other things you could do to handle the situation? Here's where you brainstorm and problem solve how to handle your fear. For example, if you spilled your drink on someone, you could pay for her dry cleaning. If you got fired from your job, you could reevaluate your priorities and turn your life around by going into a new, more satisfying job or field.

If you're worried that you won't get promoted and thus won't be able to pay your mortgage, causing the bank to foreclose on your house, think of what you can do to be sure you don't default on your mortgage. You could borrow from friends or family, take

coaching point

Go back to your list of social situations in which you felt nervous at work; pick one situation and identify how you overestimated the risk in the situation and underestimated your ability to cope. How did the situation turn out? Were you able to cope? How so? After looking at the situation, think about what a more realistic initial appraisal would have been.

out another loan, sell some of your antiques on eBay, etc. There are always possible solutions, it's just a matter of allowing yourself to see them.

Try It Out

As we've discussed, the most important step to beating anxiety is to not avoid whatever you're afraid of. Whatever you do, do *not* make an excuse about out-of-town guests keeping you from attending the office holiday party. *Don't* be the first person to leave a social gathering. *Don't* just get someone else to conduct an interview with a promising job candidate. *Don't* pretend you have a doctor's appointment to get out of going to an intimidating meeting.

Interacting well with others is one of the keys to career success. As motivational speaker and entrepreneur Jim Rohn has said, "You cannot succeed by yourself. It's hard to find a rich hermit." Continuous exposure to the social situations that make you nervous, combined with more realistic appraisals of both the risks involved and your ability to cope, will lead to decreased anxiety. I promise! There's just one exception—which brings us to our next point:

Mario's Story: Charm School

One of my executive coaching clients, Mario, jokes that being coached is like going to charm school—he learns from me how to be more charming and less annoying to his coworkers.

Mario's boss actually recommended that he enroll in coaching because he was coming across to others as abrupt, angry, and aggressive. Why? Underneath it all was a lot of anxiety about performing his best and demonstrating that he deserved his upper-level executive position. In fact, after we'd worked on some of his anxiety, a lot of his abrasive behaviors changed.

Although anxiety can make you attribute negative responses to others where none exist, sometimes there actually *are* things that you do at work that evoke negative responses in others. It's important to realize the difference. Tools like 360-degree feedback assessments can you give some good information. These 360-degree assessments are typically compiled by a coach from assessments completed by several people with whom you work (direct subordinates, bosses, coworkers). They're a great way to get a realistic understanding of how others view you at work.

If you think you could use some polishing of your social skills, why not work on them? Maybe you have a trusted friend or colleague who could give you some feedback about how you could present yourself differently. Or you could work with a professional coach or trainer. If you can find someone who understands how anxiety works—or if you can explain it to them—that would be ideal. Remember: you want to develop your skills and be aware of how you're coming across without becoming overly self-focused (which, as you know, will only increase your anxiety).

Earlier in this chapter I mentioned how intimidating conducting interviews can be when it feels strange to be the boss. Which brings us to the next chapter . . .

CHAPTER 10

You're in Charge—But You Don't Feel Like You Are

> Confidence is contagious. So is lack of confidence.
>
> —MICHAEL O'BRIEN

The Pressures of Being a Leader

Congratulations: you're a leader! Ever feel like your leadership role is tough to celebrate—or enjoy—because it's so anxiety-provoking?

In the last chapter we looked at feeling nervous around superiors, supervisors, and those who evaluate you. This chapter focuses on anxiety about *being* the supervisor or evaluator. If you're a leader, manager, or supervisor—or aspire to be one—read this chapter carefully.

Taking on the mantle of authority can be intimidating; it often ignites many of the fears and self-doubts discussed in earlier chapters. In this chapter, we'll look at some of the more common worries leadership can create and go through how to overcome them. Some people define management and leadership as separate concepts: leaders set the vision and managers implement it. For the purposes of simplicity, I use the two terms interchangeably. Whether you're a middle-level manager, a corporate leader, or you own your own business, this chapter applies to you.

The Imposter Syndrome

The imposter syndrome is something that frequently occurs for new managers and leaders. But even people who've been in leadership positions for years—or decades—may still sometimes feel like they're imposters.

Do I Deserve to Be a Leader?

A question that I frequently hear is "Who am I to be a leader?" Do you ever feel like this? Do you worry that people will find you out and the word will get around that you don't deserve to be in a leadership position?

These concerns are common among managers and directors who experience feelings of ambivalence about their leadership positions. On the one hand, you may appreciate the promotion, the salary, and all of the perks that come along with the position. On the other hand, you may be nervous and unsure if you can be effective, credible, and successful as a leader.

I Don't Know What I'm Doing!

In a position of leadership, you need to not only know what *you're* doing, but also be able to communicate to others what *they* need to be doing. But what happens when you don't know? When you're lower down on the corporate totem pole, you can always just ask someone above you. But what if the only person above you is the chief operating officer? Are you really going to ask her every time you have a question?

Part of what makes managers feel like they're imposters is the need to always act like they're on the ball. No one wants to take direction from someone who doesn't seem to know what he's doing! If you really don't know what you're doing, you may feel a need to pretend you do. While this can be a useful strategy at times, it can also be anxiety-provoking. If you're pretending all of the time, you'll always feel like you're on stage. If you have performance anxiety, this can be nerve-wracking!

You may also be managing people whose jobs you don't fully understand. This presents particular difficulties. One business owner I worked with ran a small business with a staff of only ten, and shrewdly hired people to do the things she wasn't competent to do herself. Although this is a wise business strategy, if you have no idea how to do the work yourself, overseeing it and giving feedback on it can make you very uncomfortable.

Feeling Less Than Others

If you perceive yourself as lower in social or occupational stature than those you supervise—or even those in similar positions—this too may make you feel like an imposter. As we've discussed, whenever you negatively compare yourself to someone else, anxiety is likely to result. Some of the common ways that managers evaluate themselves against their coworkers include:

Age. Ssome feel odd that they're younger than those they manage. Others feel discriminated against as older adults.

Attractiveness, height, and weight. In today's workplace, there are unfortunate biases *toward* those who are more attractive and taller—the average CEO is approximately three inches taller than the average American man (Gladwell 2005)—and *against* those who are overweight. Leaders tend to face higher levels of physical scrutiny; as a result, you may feel particularly uncomfortable about certain aspects of your physical appearance due to real or perceived biases.

Job experience. If you feel that the people you manage have more experience than you do—maybe because you've just transferred from another industry or are a relatively recent graduate—you're likely to be uncomfortable about being in charge of them. Similarly, if you're the least experienced of those in management, you may feel like you don't deserve to be among them, either.

Specific skills. If your subordinates have many specific skills that you don't, you may feel embarrassed or awkward. Since the most important and obvious skill of a leader is the ability to communicate well, if your subordinates' communication skills greatly outshine your own, you may understandably feel inferior.

coaching point

The first step to overcoming insecurity about holding a leadership position is to identify your fears. Take a few minutes to think about how you feel like an imposter or how you feel inferior as a manager or leader. What, specifically, are you lacking confidence about? What negative qualities do you worry that others may notice about you? What are you afraid might happen?

Why You're Not an Imposter

Unless you lied on your resumé or in your job interview, I can safely assure you that you're not an imposter. You're in the position you're in as a direct result of your own merit. Having utilized a connection to get that position doesn't in any way negate your merit. You deserve your job just as much as anyone else.

So why do you still feel like a fraud? If you're experiencing this imposter syndrome, you're insecure about some aspect of yourself or your work performance. The coaching point above will have uncovered what exactly you're nervous about, but remember, too, that everyone is insecure about something—either you have some area where you lack confidence or you're lying. Nobody is completely secure about every area of their work performance. Being nervous about certain aspects of your leadership position is completely normal.

In fact, having some insecurity can be beneficial. To use self-doubt effectively, you have to first determine if it's excessive. If so, is there a legitimate issue underneath the anxiety? If the insecurity is purely anxiety-driven, work to create a more realistic and less anxiety-based understanding of your work performance. Do this by looking at facts rather than how you feel at work.

Once you've identified any legitimate limitations, you can work on them through coaching, training, or mentoring. The best leaders are those who continually develop and improve. Think of the training and coaching you undertake as part of an ongoing process of improvement—*not* as a method for overcoming flaws.

The conclusion in this example is a good one: anxiety isn't the end of the world. While it may not feel comfortable, it doesn't necessarily lead to impaired performance. In fact, sometimes it helps to energize us into giving a great performance.

When Pretending Is Good

Pretending can be problematic if you're often putting pressure on yourself to give an Academy Award–winning performance. On the other hand, pretending can also be very useful. Sometimes the best way to change our beliefs is by first changing our behavior. To feel confident, you can begin by *acting* confident. When you act confident, people will respond to you in a favorable way—which will then increase your confidence. Over time, you won't need to pretend: your feelings and beliefs will align with your behavior.

coaching point

Make a page in your notebook for every concern or fear you have about your leadership abilities. Under each concern, keep a list of all the objective evidence that contradicts your fear. At the bottom of the page, write a conclusion based on the evidence that you've collected. For example:

Concern: "I feel like a phony because people think that I'm calm and collected but inside I always feel like a nervous wreck. I'm bound to break down and show everyone that I can't really cut it."

Evidence: In six years in my job, I've never broken down yet.

- Nobody has ever even mentioned that I seem tense or nervous.
- I gave a great presentation at the board meeting this week.
- My supervisor said that I'm great at motivating employees.
- I'm up for another promotion soon.

Conclusion: Even if I feel nervous, it hasn't negatively affected my work—I'm up for a promotion right now. What's the big deal about feeling nervous?

So, if you feel like an imposter and lack confidence in yourself as a leader, *try acting just a bit more confident than you are.* Good actors don't overact—so don't act as though you're way more confident than you are. This will both put too much pressure on you and come across negatively to others.

Having Authority Over Others

Being in a position of authority can be intimidating. When you're an authority figure you have many responsibilities, some of which you may not want to have.

Giving Feedback

One of the requirements of being a leader is that you oversee others and give them feedback about their performance. Receiving effective feedback is one of the most important factors in work performance. Feedback not only helps employees know what's expected and how well they're meeting these expectations, it can also make them feel valued and important. It feels good to know that our boss pays attention to our work. This is one of the things that motivates us to perform well. Besides, if our boss doesn't care, why should we?

Despite the importance of effective feedback, many managers are still hesitant to give it. Giving feedback often involves bringing up issues that you're not pleased with and that you'd like to see changed. This can be hard to do—and is likely to be especially hard with employees that you fear won't respond well.

One of my clients recently told me that he'd been putting off telling an employee he was making some errors in his proposals for weeks because he was worried about how his employee would respond.

How to Give Feedback

You may be nervous about giving feedback simply because you aren't sure how to do it. If you don't know what to do or how to frame feedback so your employee not only hears it but uses it, you're likely to feel uncomfortable.

In chapter 8 we discussed SMART goals. I think the SMART concept can also be effectively applied to giving feedback. To review, SMART goals are Specific, Measurable, Action-focused, Realistic, and Time-limited. Practice giving your feedback to employees in the form of SMART goals—after all, unless you're firing them (which we'll address in the next section), you want your feedback to move them toward certain goals or changes in their work performance.

Specific. Rather than saying, "You could work on being more sensitive at work," offer specific feedback, such as, "Your comments in yesterday's meeting were culturally insensitive because of the way that you referred to women. Some employees, both male and female, indicated that they were offended."

Measurable. Utilize measurable criteria for results. The more quantifiable your requests for change, the better—this way, both you and your employee will know when he is improving. Thus, after you and your direct subordinate come up with some ideas for change, ask, "How will we know that this improvement has occurred?"

Action-focused. Focus on specific actions as much as possible; offer potential action steps for change. The best way to accomplish this objective is to present goals as mutually constructed and beneficial. Phrases like, "What are some steps we can take to accomplish this goal?" help establish the collaborative nature of the effort—and are less likely to make your employee feel defensive.

Realistic. Before giving feedback, make sure your expectations are realistic, taking into account the individual's strengths and weaknesses as well as what can be expected given the resources and limitations of your workplace.

Time-limited. Come up with timelines for all changes and plan a follow-up meeting. Again, taking a collaborative approach can help your employee see how these changes can both benefit her career and help her accomplish her career goals.

coaching point

Identify an employee whom you'd like to give feedback to. Use the SMART format to make sure you cover all of the bases that make feedback most effective. Be sure to consider both how to get the employee's attention and help them realize how the feedback will benefit them and their career goals. Work on being constructive without being critical. Then deliver the feedback. How did it go? Did knowing an effective method to give feedback make you more confident?

Firing Employees

If you've ever had to fire or take disciplinary action against an employee, you know how difficult it is.

Jana's Story: Putting Off Letting Someone Go

My client, Jana, owned her own consulting business. She only had five employees. One of them, a receptionist, was simply not cutting it. After several attempts at giving feedback and making plans for change, it was clear to Jana that the woman needed to be fired. Because my client knew this woman was a single mother of three kids, she felt bad about letting her go—so bad that she put it off for months. Meanwhile, her business was losing money because she had an ineffective employee interacting with clients.

We've talked a lot about how avoidance increases anxiety. This was definitely the case with Jana: the more she put off firing her employee, the more she worried about it. She intended to do it in the fall but put it off. Then it was the holidays and she felt bad about firing her then. If she had only done it when she first decided to, it would have been a lot easier.

Conducting Interviews

As we discussed in the last chapter, conducting an interview can be difficult—you need to represent the company in a positive way, appear professional and knowledgeable, and ask the interviewee good questions. If your boss has already decided that she wants to hire the candidate, you may also face a lot of pressure from her.

Another potential difficulty with conducting interviews is that the candidate may be nervous. Being around someone who is anxious can make *you* more anxious. Although you may try hard to put them at ease or help them to feel comfortable, this puts pressure on you and as a result you're more likely to feel self-conscious.

The other aspect of conducting interviews that makes many managers uncomfortable is being asked questions about the job or the company by the interviewee. As we discussed in chapter 5, having to answer questions frequently brings up performance anxiety.

Managing Conflict

If you aren't anxious to begin with, you may still become anxious if you find yourself caught up in employee conflict—it's distressing to be in a tense atmosphere in which people are clashing.

You're in Charge

When you're the leader, it's your job to keep your team performing well. When there is conflict, people can get distracted by the drama and neglect their responsibilities. Moreover, disagreements may not only take people off task, they can reduce morale and hinder employees' confidence in you as a leader.

Managing Conflict Before It Manages You

The first step to managing conflict in your work team is to understand where it's coming from. What's fueling it? Is it a matter of employee personality clashes? Are employees under a good deal of stress due to tight deadlines or limited resources? Are people unsure of their job descriptions and stepping on each other's toes?

A very common source of conflict is problems with how work has been delegated. (More about delegation in the next section.) Another common source of employee conflict is the allocation of limited resources. Occasionally, the heart of the problem is simply one or two employees who are difficult to work with or who don't pull their weight.

The second step in managing conflict is to plan your intervention. Ask yourself, "What can I do to diffuse conflict and get emotions under control?" You want to bring the level of animosity or stress down so people can effectively address the issue at hand. Jumping into problem solving without first diffusing tension can be ineffective if people are still too frustrated to think proactively. This is like kids who have been fighting: often you need to split them up so they can calm down before you talk to them about why they were fighting.

Also, as you plan your intervention, you need to identify *how* you're going to help sort out the difficulties. You may decide to meet with your employees individually. You may decide to change how projects have been delegated or resources allocated. Or you may decide to shuffle the team around or change the distribution of labor dramatically.

The third step is to implement the intervention you've decided on. If you're nervous about doing this, you may want to discuss your plan with a colleague first. Anticipate the objections and difficulties that are likely to come up and prepare for them. However, as in any interaction, don't overrehearse or overplan to the point of allowing the preparation to become an overcompensating behavior.

The last step is to follow up—meet with your team and with the feuding employees regularly to be sure your intervention is working. Make sure that your employees know the specific steps to take to keep the conflict under control; if someone refuses to cooperate, be sure they know the potential consequences of their actions.

coaching point

Think about a current workplace conflict. How can you use the above steps to manage the situation? Make a specific action plan. If you don't have a current experience, think about a past experience. What could you have done to better handle the conflict? What did you do well? If you were ever the employee in a disagreement or conflict, think about how your manager handled it. What did and didn't work?

Assertive Communication

Being able to communicate assertively means that you can state your opinion even if it's in contrast to another's. You can ask for help when you need it or ask someone to do something differently than they have been. You can also say no and refuse to take on additional work and responsibilities. According to Randy Paterson, author of *The Assertiveness Workbook: How to Express Your Ideas and Stand Up for Yourself at Work and in Relationships* (2000), the key to speaking assertively is that you aren't aggressive and you aren't passive, but instead you're both respectful to others and in control of your own behavior.

Anxiety and a lack of assertiveness are linked in several ways. For example, let's say that you have perfectionist tendencies and worry about producing suboptimal work. If you aren't able to say no to certain projects, you'll quickly become overwhelmed—and more nervous about completing your tasks well.

Some perfectionists also have difficulty asking for assistance even when it's very reasonable to get assistance. This is because your perfectionist tendencies make you feel like you *should* be able to do everything on your own. Developing assertiveness can help you get the assistance you need to overcome perfectionism and do your job well.

Making Requests

There are three key steps to making requests in an assertive manner. First, state the reason the request would be beneficial. Second, ask for the specific item that you want. Third, arrange a specific plan to implement your request. Always consider what's in it for the person you're speaking to; have empathy for their position. (You can vary the order of steps two and three based on the specific request.)

For example, "Jim, I know that our account with Fadar is extremely important. For this reason, I'm putting my all into it. But I'm having difficulty moving forward without the data I need. I'd like about three hours of time from one of the assistants. Once they get the data to me, I can move forward quickly. Can I have three hours from one of the assistants this week? What day should I plan on?"

Saying No

Saying no can be very difficult, especially when you're trying to show your company that you are extremely dedicated and hard-working. For this reason, it's important to clarify why you're saying no. Again, always consider what's in it for the other person—they're likely to be displeased with your refusal of their request, so it's important to highlight any ways your refusal might benefit them.

For example, "I got the new assignment that you sent. I'm actually still working on the project that you said is the number one priority this quarter. The completion of that project is likely to land the million-dollar account and generate leads to at least ten new projects. I'd suggest that I focus my efforts on finishing that project before taking on something new. I'll have it completed by next Friday. How does that sound?"

Delegating

The types of requests discussed above typically arise when you're asking for something from your boss or supervisor. Making requests of your subordinates is typically a type of delegation. As you may know, successful delegation is a mixture of science and art.

Employees are most motivated when they feel invested in the project or role that they're assigned to. When you delegate, you want to keep this in mind. One way to encourage this is by allowing employees to choose among several activities. Choice gives people the perception of control and helps involve them in the process. Or you can highlight the specific skills and attributes of the individual that make them well-suited to the task at hand. People typically perform in line with the expectations and feedback that others give them—when you highlight the positive qualities of an individual and say why you expect them to do well, you set up a beneficial self-fulfilling prophecy.

The art of delegation comes in here because you want to provide support and feedback without micromanaging. If you have ever been micromanaged, you know how annoying and demoralizing it is. It's also anxiety-provoking: you feel like someone is watching over you and evaluating your every move. Many perfectionist managers have a difficult time delegating and not micromanaging because it requires giving up some control. Remember that although your anxiety may make you want to control work situations, the more you control, the more others will resist—making you less effective and raising your anxiety. You want to earn respect as a leader and have people *want* to listen to you, not feel that they have to because you're standing over their shoulders and micromanaging.

A good leader provides employees with the resources and feedback they need to perform well. Build in systems for monitoring the progress of employees. Work hard to empower them both to excel and to ask for assistance when needed.

Sheila's Story: The Broken Record

My client Sheila, a mid-level executive, had an employee who continuously complained about a coworker. In Sheila's view—and in the view of other team members—he employee simply had a personality clash with the other individual. Sheila had a talk with this employee during which she carefully listened to the employee's issues and offered some suggestions and plans to diffuse the tension; she also let her employee know that her complaints were hurting team morale. Sheila and her employee decided to try some of the suggestions for six weeks; if there was still conflict, the work team would then need to be reshuffled.

Sheila had handled the situation assertively and proactively; there was no longer any reason for the employee to continue to complain to her. Yet the employee continued to complain. To combat this, Sheila began using the broken record technique: every time the employee complained, Sheila replied, "Focus on your job and not how much she bothers you." (If you have kids, you've probably used this technique.) Over time, the employee finally got the message and stopped complaining.

Women in Leadership

Top female executives or business owners sometimes face additional anxiety about being in a leadership role. In part, this is because there are fewer women than men in upper-level executive positions. When you're seen as representing women as a whole, you can feel as though there's a lot of pressure on you. You can also feel like you are in the spotlight. This is particularly true in some industries, like technology and finance.

Journalist Del Jones, in an article for *USA Today* in 2003, pointed out that only eight of the CEOs of Fortune 500 companies are women. (Interestingly, the companies that these eight women headed significantly outperformed other companies in 2003.) Imagine being one of those eight women! I, personally, would feel a lot of pressure to represent women well.

Some of the female executives I've worked with say that they receive a lot of mixed messages from their workplaces. If they look or act "too feminine," they get criticized as being too soft. If they look or act "too masculine," they're described as too tough, cold, or bitchy. If you're already somewhat prone to feeling anxious, the additional burden and confusion of all this pressure and these mixed messages can be a recipe for being anxious nine to five.

Psychologist Priscilla Marotta (1999) proposes several stages of coaching for executive women. These stages include: overcoming negative perceptions of power, adding positive perceptions of power, exploring the effects of socialization and gender myths, and networking to increase resources.

coaching point

This coaching exercise is for women in business. Self-coach yourself through Marotta's stages of coaching. Begin by examining any negative perceptions you have of having power and control. Then think about why being in a position of power is a good thing. Explore how aspects of how you were raised may have impacted your thinking about being in a leadership position. For example, women are often socialized to maintain peace and harmony in groups—how might this affect your abilities to deal with conflict? Write down any gender myths or mixed messages you've encountered. Finally, make a list of ten ways that you can effectively network. Consider networking opportunities both inside and outside your current organization.

Anxiety-Free Leadership

If you're a leader—or you plan to be someday—use the principles in this book and have confidence in yourself and your abilities as a leader. Confidence is one of the best cures for beating anxiety and enjoying a leadership role. (We'll talk more about ways to increase confidence in chapter 12.)

Don't be inhibited by your anxiety. Push yourself to do something you're uncomfortable about every day. Take some risks and work on leaving a legacy in your career. As Ralph Waldo Emerson said, "Do not go where the path may lead, go instead where there is no path and leave a trail."

CHAPTER 11

The Workplace Worrier

> I try not to worry about the future—so I take each day just one anxiety attack at a time.
>
> —TOM WILSON

Borrowing Problems

Do you worry about the many roadblocks and difficulties that might arise in your job? Are you frequently borrowing future problems? If you're busy predicting far out into the future, you may find yourself worrying about something so far down the line that it's unlikely to even occur.

Worry creates monsters out of shadows. When you worry, you become focused on potential danger, embarrassment, or other negative events. At the same time, you're likely to become less able to focus on how you would handle any difficult event that might arise. As you read through this chapter, keep the formula for anxiety in mind:

Overestimation of Risk

\+ = Anxiety

Underestimation of Ability to Cope

Worrying as a Liability

I like the phrase "borrowing problems"—worrying is a lot like borrowing money. Just as a loan is a liability, worrying is a liability. Worrying costs you time, energy, performance, and sometimes even relationships. It reduces your enjoyment in things and increases your anxiety level.

In its severe form, worrying can be a symptom of an anxiety disorder, such as obsessive-compulsive disorder (OCD) or generalized anxiety disorder (GAD). Obsessive-compulsive disorder typically involves worries that are unremitting, highly distressing, and repetitive accompanied by compulsive behaviors intended to reduce this anxiety. Generalized anxiety disorder, known as the "worry disease," typically exhibits as chronic excessive worry, muscle tension, and concentration difficulties. If you think that your worrying is significantly impairing your functioning, seek out a psychological evaluation (see the resources section on finding referrals).

Worrying as an Asset

Many people who worry don't believe that worrying is a liability, but believe it actually helps them. You may think, "Worrying keeps me on my toes," or, "Worrying helps me to anticipate negative events and plan for them," or even, "I might forget things if I didn't worry about them." Thus, though part of you may realize that your worrying causes anxiety, another part of you may think worrying also helps you out. This is one of the reasons that worry sticks around and can be difficult to get rid of.

Second-Guessing

We discussed second-guessing as an avoidance strategy in chapter 8. Second-guessing is also both a major cause and result of worry. For example, if you're a marketing executive and you make the decision to select one advertising campaign over another, you may then begin to worry about whether you made the right decision. "What if this campaign is too controversial?" you might think. "I may have sacrificed an excellent campaign that wouldn't offend anyone in favor of a campaign that may tarnish our brand . . . What if my boss thinks I have poor judgment and I'm not worthy of my position?"

The more you worry about it, the more you second-guess yourself. Likewise, once you start second-guessing yourself, you begin the snowball process of worry. One of the reasons that worrying makes you second-guess yourself is that it puts you into an anxious mind-set in which you're less rational and objective. It can also interfere with your attention and concentration, making you more likely to either forget whether you did something or doubt whether you did it well.

Rework the Worry Formula

Remember the equation for anxiety I described above? In this section, I'll teach you the keys to reversing this formula to create a formula for control and confidence instead of worry and anxiety.

"It Feels So Likely to Happen . . ."

You may simply overestimate the likelihood of a threat occurring. For example, you may feel it's highly likely that your boss is going to hate your proposal or that you won't get the job you're interviewing for or that you'll make a fool of yourself when you present at the next meeting. Counter this concern by realizing that just because it *feels* likely does not mean it *is* likely.

"The Outcome Could Be Horrible . . ."

Do you have a very imaginative and creative mind, a mind that automatically conjures up worries and imagines all sorts of negative possibilities? In my experience, people who are prone to worrying tend to be highly intelligent, inventive individuals—this is one of the reasons I enjoy working with people with anxiety so much. Think about it—you do have to be imaginative and bright to come up with some of your worries!

When people worry excessively, they often imagine catastrophic outcomes that could occur. Horrible outcomes tend to be more mentally compelling—and thus make worries more persistent. But just how horrible would it be if your worry came true? Try these exercises to find out.

coaching point

1. In your notebook, write a story about the most horrible thing that could happen. Go through all of the details of this catastrophe. You might write something like: "I'll say something ridiculous and my coworkers will lose all respect for me. As a result, they won't listen to any of my directions and ideas when I'm the lead on team projects. My boss won't promote me and eventually I won't earn enough money to support my family. My kids won't get healthy food to eat and won't go to college. Instead, they'll end up uneducated and angry at me for ruining their lives."

2. Can you see how the train of worries starts going out of control? It starts speeding along and winds up in Unrealistic-ville. Identify this in your own worry, too.

3. Once you see how unrealistic your worry's ultimate feared outcome really is, create a new, more realistic assessment of what might happen if the worry did come true. For example, "I'll say something ridiculous and feel very embarrassed. People may be surprised by how silly my statement is. I'll probably feel embarrassed around coworkers for the rest of the day. But they'll probably forget about it, maybe in an hour or at least by the end of the day. I may take a little longer to forget about it, but I will when I see no one treats me any differently."

"I Couldn't Handle That"

It's important to realize three things: that your worries aren't as likely to happen as you may think, that outcomes aren't as catastrophic as they originally appear, and that you can handle the outcomes that do occur. This last point addresses the second variable of the anxiety equation: your underestimation of your ability to cope with the difficult situation. We humans have an incredible capacity to cope with adversity. Typically, the anxiety involved in anticipating a difficult situation is worse than the problems we actually experience in the situation.

A Paradoxical Approach

One way to help you tap into your ability to cope is by taking a paradoxical, reverse psychology approach with yourself. Play devil's advocate. Tell yourself, "Well, now I'm just going to lie down and wallow in the grief from the situation and do nothing to change it."

When you take this approach, you bring out the stronger side of yourself in response. We all have strong sides and weak sides to our personalities. Coaching helps you to tap into your strong side. Throughout this book, I've been helping you to be your own coach and ask yourself the questions that lead to a decrease in anxiety and increase in self-confidence. The idea here is to provoke a response similar to what happens when you hear someone insult your spouse, your child, or your parent. You can complain about them all you want, but someone else says the same thing and it's, "Hey! Wait a minute there!" The same effect happens when you take a paradoxical approach with yourself and say, "Well, I guess there's no way I could possibly cope with that situation." Almost immediately you'll begin to think of ways that you *can* cope.

One caveat to this approach: don't use it if you are in the midst of serious depression or anxiety. If you're experiencing significant anxiety, allow it to naturally subside or habituate to it before trying this paradoxical approach. When people are depressed, they feel hopeless and unable to see the positive side of things; in this situation, a reverse psychology approach could feed the depression. However, cognitive behavioral therapies are very effective in treating depression; get the treatment you need first, then try this approach.

Finding Solutions to the Problem

Another way to develop a more realistic estimation of your ability to cope with the consequences of your worry is to problem solve. To problem solve effectively, you need to first separate the aspects of your worry about which you have control from those aspects that are beyond your control. Let's say you worry about a corporate merger resulting in a large number of layoffs in your company. The first step is to *accept* the fact that you have no control over whether the merger and layoffs occur. Worrying is often completely futile—we often waste time worrying about things that we have virtually no control over. The way to handle this is to simply accept your lack of control.

The next step is to problem solve. What if you did get laid off? What would you do then? Problem solving involves creating a series of steps or options that you could take in the event that your worry comes true. For example, you could plan how to tap into your networks, both inside and outside your company. You could use the layoff as an impetus to move to a new city you've been wanting to live in. Or you could use the layoff to propel you into the self-employment you've longed for.

When you problem solve, you learn that not only can you handle the potential problem, but the problem itself might actually present a wonderful opportunity. Some of the most successful businesspeople in the world didn't become successful until they were presented with problems they had to overcome. Walt Disney, for example, went from bankruptcy to building the Disney empire. Several of my entrepreneurial coaching clients used job layoffs as the impetus to begin businesses that turned into multimillion-dollar companies.

Problems and opportunity are two sides of the same coin. When you toss it and it lands on problems, flip it over.

coaching point

Next time you find yourself worrying, use the paradoxical approach and problem solving to deal with your worry. Tell yourself, "Surely I can't handle this." Once you realize, "Yes, actually, there are things I can do," ask yourself what those things are. Brainstorm a list of coping strategies and problem solving steps that you can take.

Worry Exposure

We've discussed how anxiety typically increases when you try to push it away but decreases when you allow yourself to experience it. Think of pushing down worry like bouncing a ball: the more you push it down, the more it bounces back up. The harder you push it down, the higher it will go. What do you think happens if you stopped bouncing the ball back down? It would continue to bounce, but with less force each time. The same idea holds true for worry—when you allow it to just exist, without trying to force it down, it will go down on its own. But if you stop pushing the ball down and then run away, you wouldn't see that it stops bouncing. The key is to allow the worry to be there and then to stick with it until you see that it goes down.

Scheduling Worry Time

One solution to excessive worrying is to worry on purpose. I know, it sounds crazy, but it works. It can also help you worry in a more productive manner. When a worry pops up, you may not be ready for it. By scheduling when to worry, you can control it—it won't control you.

coaching point

Try this exercise: As hard as you can, try *not* to imagine a pink elephant. Don't think of a pink elephant and don't create a mental picture of one. What happens? You see the pink elephant, right? Now, try *to* picture the pink elephant in your mind. Keep it there for five minutes. Don't picture anything else, just see the pink elephant clearly. What happens? It's hard to keep it there, right? Purposefully thinking about something can actually help your mind to get rid of it. You can only think about something for so long, so why not think about it at a time that's convenient?

Ellen's Story: Wearing Your Worries Out

At forty, Ellen, a successful architect, had difficulty sleeping—she'd lie awake at night worrying about the things she needed to do and the difficulties that might arise the next day. She tried to force herself to push her worries away, but they were persistent: no matter how hard she tried to ignore them and just go to sleep, they kept coming back. Ellen became sleep-deprived and increasingly anxious about her work. She even began to avoid going to bed because it was such an unpleasant experience. Instead she'd stay up and clean, work, or do other things. Her worries started to become self-fulfilling—because they were sapping her energy, motivation, and confidence, she was beginning to perform less well on the job.

I gave Ellen a crazy assignment: purposefully worry at a designated time each day. We picked 7–7:45 P.M., right after she got home from work but far enough from bedtime that her worries wouldn't interfere with her sleep. By worrying earlier in the day, by the time bedtime rolled around her mind was already done with its worrying. If a worry popped up before bed, Ellen would just think, "Been there, done that, over it" since she'd already thought through her worries.

One of the reasons scheduling worrying worked so well for Ellen was that it helped her gain new perspective on her worries. Engaging in productive worrying helped her sort out which worries she had no control over and which worries she could brainstorm solutions for.

Ellen learned to talk back to her worries when they popped up later in the evening. When a worry popped up about something she couldn't control, she'd think, "I can't do anything about that, so it's a waste of time to even think about it." And when a worry popped up that she'd already come up with solutions for, she simply reminded herself that she'd already thought about that one and was ready for it.

Postponing Worries—Procrastination That's Okay

We've talked a lot about how procrastination and avoidance can enable anxiety. One exception to this rule is purposefully procrastinating your worrying—e.g., telling yourself that you'll postpone your worrying about something until a later point in time.

In the case study above, whenever Ellen found herself worrying before her scheduled worrying time, she'd write her concern down in a notebook and then put it away until the worry time. When a worry came up again after her worry time, Ellen would talk back to it as described above. If a new worry popped up after the worry time, she'd write it down in the notebook and postpone it until the next day.

One of the reasons that this postponing practice is so effective is that it actually proves to you that you're in control of the worrying. Another reason is that it removes you from the cycle of endlessly pushing it away only to have it fight back. Instead, you acknowledge it and deal with it proactively—at the time of day that works best for you. As a result, you'll no longer be distracted from your work or your fun by worrying.

Stay in the Moment

Stop borrowing problems by keeping yourself grounded firmly in the present. Worrying involves thinking about future difficulties and problems—if you're truly focused on the present moment, it will be impossible to worry.

Mindfulness Training

Becoming truly present in the present moment requires *mindfulness.* Mindfulness is a nonjudgmental focus on what is happening in the here and now: you don't hold onto the good and you don't try to push away the bad. As Holly Hazlett-Stevens points out in *Women Who Worry Too Much* (2005), the goal of mindfulness training is both to move you out of your worries and into the experience at hand, and to allow you to experience what comes your way without judgment or worry about "bad" outcomes.

When to Involve Others

Are you someone who often involves others in your worrying? If you frequently talk about your worries or ask people for reassurance, then knowing how to rely on others healthily will be helpful to you. Think of worry as a nagging child who wants to be the center of attention. The more adults respond to him, the more his

coaching point

A wonderful thing about mindfulness training is that to do it, you don't need to steal away any additional time from your busy day. Practicing mindfulness through meditation is highly valuable, but you can also do any activity in a mindful way. For example, if you're washing the dishes, experience the moment: take in the feeling of the water, notice the color of the plates, listen to the sound of running water. If you're going for a walk, observe the feeling of the ground beneath your feet, feel the crispness of the air, hear the noises around you.

After you've practiced mindful attention outside of work, practice it in your office, too. If you're under stress and prone to beginning the cycle of worry, focus your attention on what you're doing in the moment. When you live nonjudgmentally in the moment, you don't place an opinion on what you're doing, you simply experience it. Allow yourself to become fully immersed and engaged. This practice also helps you to improve your focus and attention, thereby increasing the quality and quantity of your work.

nagging will be reinforced. Similarly, when you get worked up and pull others into your worries, your worrying and second-guessing gets reinforced. For this reason, it's typically not a good idea to continuously ask for reassurance or vent nonstop to others.

On the other hand, it can be useful to have others help you problem solve and brainstorm. To do this effectively, first identify whether your worry is of the unproductive/uncontrollable variety or of the productive/controllable variety. If it's of the uncontrollable variety, don't ask for reassurance—people can't give you any real reassurance about things that are unpredictable anyway. If it's a worry that you *can* control, you can get useful support from others to help with your problem solving. Just be careful to work on improving this skill on your own as well.

Another very important way that you can involve others in helping you overcome workplace worry is to do enjoyable things with them. Relaxation and enjoyment can help you beat the worrying cycle. Which brings us to the next point.

Relaxation and Stress Management

Stress is different from anxiety or worry. Stress has to do with external pressures and difficulties whereas anxiety is an internal type of pressure. Stress can, however, lead to increased worrying: it saps your coping capabilities and makes you more susceptible to allowing your worrying to spiral out of control. For this reason, activities that help you to relax and de-stress can be very useful. I'll describe some common stress management and relaxation exercises, but feel free to try other things on your own to see what works for you.

Deep Breathing for De-Stressing

When stressed and anxious, we're prone to taking rapid, shallow breaths from the chest. This type of shallow, quick breathing can actually stimulate your nervous system to become even more aroused. This shallow breathing can be either a cause or a result of anxiety. Some people begin breathing shallowly and then experience physical signs of anxiety, triggering them to become even more anxious. Others find that they begin to breathe more shallowly when they feel anxious over an extended period of time. Regardless of which is more typical for you, the solution is the same: take deep breaths from the diaphragm to trigger relaxation instead of anxiety.

coaching point

Deep breathing takes practice. Over time, you'll be able to use deep breathing to relax you when you're anxious. Practice deep breathing at times when you're not keyed up or nervous. Begin by placing your hand over your stomach. As you inhale, your hand should rise and fall (a sign that you're breathing from the diaphragm and not the chest). Slowly inhale through your nose for a count of four. Then exhale through either your nose or mouth for another slow count of four. When you exhale, say a calming word like "relax."

Guided Imagery

If you're someone who is good at creating mental images, you can use your imagination to your advantage by guiding yourself through positive imagery. What we see around us is directly linked to our feelings—you feel differently when you're walking in a bright, sunny meadow full of beautiful spring wildflowers than you do when you're sitting in your cubicle under a harsh fluorescent light. Giving yourself a mental vacation from stress and worry can be as effective as giving yourself a real vacation.

Progressive Muscle Relaxation

When you worry a great deal, your body often becomes tense and your muscles cramp up. This muscle tension keeps your body on edge; by being physically wound up and prepped for a fight-or-flight response, your body signals danger to your brain. Learning to relax your muscles helps your body become at ease and your mind overcome anxiety.

coaching point

Practice this imagery at home when you're already somewhat relaxed. As you get used to doing it, you can call upon it during stressful moments at work to help you stay calm and worry-free.

1. First, close your eyes and practice the deep breathing described above.
2. Then, think about one of the times in your life when you were very relaxed, happy, and free of worry. This could be a childhood memory or a recent vacation; you can even use an upcoming vacation if you can picture what it'll look like. Outdoor images—like lying on a Mediterranean beach, sitting in a cool forest, or having a picnic in a field—are often relaxing.
3. Next, imagine yourself reexperiencing your memory. Use your senses to feel the warmth of the sun, smell the fresh grass, or see the crystal blue of the water. Hold yourself in this image as you feel yourself relax. Stay with it for several minutes before opening your eyes.
4. When you return to your activities, bring this feeling of calmness and contentment with you.

The best way to relax your muscles is actually by tensing them first. This may sound counterintuitive, but it works because it helps you become aware of your natural muscle tension; it also helps you recognize the difference between tense and relaxed. It's like going down a big hill as opposed to a little hill—the way down

coaching point

Here's a brief muscle relaxation that you can use to relax your muscles at work or at home (Bernstein, Borkovec, and Hazlett-Stevens 2000). Try to practice it twice a day, for fifteen minutes each time. Tense a group of muscles (see list below) and hold the tension in those muscles for seven seconds. Release the tension quickly. Notice the difference in the way you feel when the muscles are relaxed. Enjoy the relaxed feeling for about thirty seconds and then tense the next muscle group. Follow the muscle groups in this order:

The facial muscles. Begin with your face: furrow your brow, clench your jaw, tightly close your eyes.

The muscles in your arms, neck, and shoulders. Hold your arms out in front of you, bend them, make fists. Pull your shoulders up to your ears and tighten all muscles in your arms.

The chest and stomach. Hold your breath and suck in your stomach (as if someone just punched you in the stomach).

The thigh muscles. Sitting in a chair, raise your legs up. Use the top muscles of your legs to push them back down.

Lower legs and foot muscles. Flex your feet upward; tighten the calf muscles.

is more noticeable and powerful with the big hill. If you tense up first, the relaxing release of the muscles is also more intense.

Exercise the Worries Away

I recommend regular exercise to all of my clients. When you're prone to anxiety, exercise is particularly important. Exercise can keep worry from snowballing. Exercise can calm you down and prevent worry from beginning. Exercise works as a natural medication, in many ways similar to the medications typically prescribed for anxiety. In *Coping with Anxiety: 10 Simple Ways to Relieve Anxiety, Fear, and Worry* (2003), authors Edmund Bourne and Lorna Garano point out some of the many biological benefits that regular aerobic activity bestows, including:

- Reduced muscle tension
- Faster metabolism of adrenaline (gets you out of the fight-or-flight response more quickly)
- Increased production of endorphins (substances that makes you feel better)
- Stimulation of serotonin (decreases depression and anxiety)
- Increased acidity (lower pH) of the blood (increases your energy)

Exercise can also lead to weight loss, improved sleep, and strengthened muscle tone, all of which can increase your confidence and make you less susceptible to worry.

If you're going to exercise to reduce worry, make sure you're doing it the right way. (Aerobic activity is typically the best way to experience the benefits described above.) Create a schedule that you can stick to, since regular exercise (three to four times per week) maximizes the benefits you'll receive. Anticipate and problem solve any difficulty or excuse that may get in your way. Make sure that you're not using your exercise time to worry. Select an activity that is engaging enough that it's easy to stay mindful and present-focused. Fitness classes, mountain biking, swimming, and martial arts are all good examples of engaging activities that can give your mind a break from worrying.

Eat Right to Fight Worry

You probably know all about the benefits of eating a well-balanced diet. But did you know that the way you eat can also help you to reduce anxiety?

You may have noticed that caffeine can make you feel nervous or jittery. This is because caffeine stimulates sympathetic nervous system activity (our fight-or-flight response is triggered in the same way) and increases the level of a neurotransmitter called epinephrine in your brain. As a result, your body is on alert—and you become more susceptible to worry and anxiety. Caffeine also depletes the antistress vitamin thiamine, or B_1. The amount of caffeine it's okay to have each day varies by individual, but most people should have less than 100mg per day (Bourne and Garano 2003).

Begin monitoring the caffeine in your food and drinks; be aware that when you order decaf you can never know exactly how decaffeinated it is. Also examine over-the-counter medications for headaches, dieting, premenstrual syndrome, and staying awake to see if caffeine is an ingredient.

Another major anxiety culprit is sugar. When you eat too many foods containing a high amount of simple sugar, the sugar level in your blood becomes deregulated. Hypoglycemia can result. Symptoms of hypoglycemia—feeling light-headed or unsteady, trembling, or heart palpitations—mimic anxiety and can trigger anxiety responses as a result. To prevent this cycle altogether, decrease the amount of simple sugars such as white sugar, high fructose corn syrup, and dextrose in your diet. Simultaneously work on adding complex carbohydrates (like whole wheat pasta) and protein to your diet. Also, regulate your blood sugar level by eating at equal intervals throughout the day.

coaching point

Begin regulating your diet first by monitoring what you're eating. Once you see patterns emerge, you can begin making eliminations and substitutions. If you have a lot of caffeine in your diet, reduce it gradually—e.g., eliminate one cup of coffee a day, or have a cup of half decaf and half regular coffee. If you find that you typically reach for a cup of coffee or a sugary snack around three P.M., eat a snack that combines a protein with a complex carbohydrate (like peanut butter on whole wheat toast or cheese on wheat crackers) just before three. Also, look for opportunities to reduce acid-forming foods like meat, poultry, and dairy products in favor of vegetables, fruits, and whole grains. Notice the difference in the changes you make in terms of the anxiety, energy, and worry you feel.

Worry-Free and Ready for Career Success

With fewer worries demanding your attention, you can concentrate on career advancement. If worries continue to pop up, allow them to just be there and float away on their own, and then refocus yourself on where you want to get *to* (not away from). Commit to putting the ideas from this chapter into practice; don't allow worry to hold you back from your goals.

The next chapter is the most important one in the book: it helps you build your self-assurance and create the most successful career possible. Ready to turn your confidence, work performance, and career up a notch? If so, turn the page to our last chapter!

CHAPTER 12

Your Confidence and Career Success

> To become successful is to recognize every tiny step toward success—and then take more of them.
>
> —LARINA KASE

Creating Success

I'd like you to approach this chapter with the awareness that you're beginning a new chapter in your life. With anxiety around, you were probably very focused on worries, problems, and potential failures. Now is the time to focus on success—even the tiny little steps that work together to take you where you want to go. Anxiety expected bad things to happen; but you're ready to expect good things now.

My goal for you isn't simply to overcome workplace anxiety. I want you to use the principles we've discussed to develop confidence and enjoy a highly successful career. Now that you've learned how to keep your anxiety in line, you're in a great position to push yourself to try new things, take some risks, and soar to the top of your field!

Understand Biases

Both the behaviors we exhibit and the interpretations we put on things are very much influenced by biases. By understanding these biases, you can not only help yourself overcome anxiety and create realistic appraisals of workplace situations, you can also recognize biases in yourself and others and use them in your favor.

Remember the Self-Fulfilling Prophecy

We've talked a lot about self-fulfilling prophecies: when you think something is true—or will be true in the future—you end up acting in ways that make it true. There's been a lot of interesting research on this concept. For example, in one study, researchers showed male participants a photo of the woman they were about to talk to on the phone (Snyder, Tank, and Berscheid 1977). In reality, of course, the picture—either of an attractive woman or an unattractive woman—was chosen by the experimenters, and wasn't actually the woman the participants talked to. When the men thought the woman they were speaking to was attractive, the woman's voice came across as more friendly, likeable, and sociable as rated by objective listeners. This was because the men talked differently to the women they thought were attractive and unattractive—and then the way the men spoke affected the way the woman on the other end of the phone responded.

Be aware of what you think is going to happen: it's probably going to happen—because you make it happen. This can work against you, or it can work for you. It's your choice.

It works against you when you expect the worst. If you have an upcoming presentation and you think to yourself, "It's going to be horrible, I'll make a fool of myself," guess what? Your fears will probably come true. Work on creating positive expectations of success instead.

Mental Rehearsal

One very powerful and effective way of creating a self-fulfilling prophecy that will work for you instead of against you is to use mental rehearsal. We've talked about how you may use mental rehearsal negatively, as an overcompensating behavior—how it can actually redirect your attention to yourself and make you more self-conscious. Well, there's another, healthy, helpful way to use mental rehearsal: to positively imagine success. This is something that Olympic athletes, Academy Award–winning actors, and other high performers do. It works. The goal is to walk yourself through a fantastic performance in your mind. Picture what you'll look like, how you'll feel, how others will respond to you, and the results of your incredible performance.

This strategy works particularly well for presentations, meeting new people, important proposals and projects, and other performance situations. The best time to practice is in advance of your performance. When you're in the actual situation, you want to focus all of your energy on the performance or conversation—not be in your mind. Give yourself the right mind-set for optimal performance—then once you're in it, go for it!

coaching point

Try this experiment: give two talks. The first time, before you speak, think carefully about all of the things you could do wrong. Picture the worst that could happen. See yourself as awkward, unattractive, and definitely not poised. As you speak, focus on your flaws and all those parts of yourself that you want to hide.

Give another talk a day later. If possible, speak in front of the same people. This time, picture yourself as poised, confident, and attractive. Close your eyes and see yourself speaking clearly and calmly. See others responding to you with smiles and nods. Feel the pride of a great talk when you finish. Then open your eyes and speak. Notice the differences in how you felt the first time versus the second time. Which talk was more natural, enjoyable, and well received?

The Fundamental Attribution Bias

You see your boss make a face while you're presenting; you notice that one of your team members appears annoyed and leaves the room while you're speaking. If you're like most of us, you'll automatically assume that these behaviors are related to your speaking. For example, you may assume that your boss is making a face because of his dissatisfaction with what you're saying; of course, in reality, he may be thinking about how one of his stocks just plummeted. Or you may think that your teammate is leaving the room because he can't stand the sound of your voice, when really he's been paged with a family emergency.

These situations exemplify our *fundamental attribution bias*. Research backs this up: A study by Edward Jones in 1979 showed that we tend to assume that people's behaviors are driven by internal dispositions rather than external situations. Moreover, research by Nisbett and Ross (1980) suggests that we attribute causality to the most salient feature of a situation—and the most salient features are typically observable actions rather than the situation or context in which they occur.

coaching point

Catch yourself when you make this attribution error; recognize that you're assuming that a negative response is an internal reaction to you, rather than something that may be going on external to both of you. Think of some times when you've made this type of attribution in the past; consider potential situational or external explanations for others' behavior in these situations.

The Self-Serving Bias

You may need to develop more of a *self-serving bias*. A self-serving bias is the tendency to attribute positive results to internal factors and negative results to external factors like chance or the difficulty of the task (Kelley 1973). This protective bias can help us become more optimistic and successful.

Without this bias, people are prone to frustration and depression; without this bias, people are more likely to believe that they're responsible for every mistake or failure and overlook some of the external factors that may be responsible. Additionally, without this bias, people may feel their successes are due to luck or a fluke and won't feel in control of creating more success.

When you help yourself develop internal explanations for success and see negative events as time-limited and specific to a situation (as opposed to global in nature), you create what researcher Martin Seligman calls *learned optimism* (1991). Studies suggest that optimists outperform pessimists in sports, sales, and stress management. One reason for this is that optimists have a vision of success. We'll discuss this idea more in the next section, but first, try this coaching point:

coaching point

Create learned optimism by practicing attributing your successes to internal, stable, and global factors and your failures to external, unstable, and specific factors. (Don't worry, you won't shirk responsibility by doing this, rather you'll learn a more optimistic approach to balance out your tendency toward anxiety and anticipating the worst.)

For example, if you learned that your company didn't get a project you were in charge of proposing to a client, the pessimistic way to view the situation would be: "It's all my fault!" (internal); "I'm never adequately prepared . . ." (stable); and, "I'll probably lose the next account too" (global). In your notebook, turn these pessimistic attributions around; write the opposite responses to help you see other possibilities. For example: "The customer is looking for a larger company to suit their needs" (external); "I've landed several great accounts in the past" (unstable); and, "This is just one proposal, and we weren't a good match for the customer" (specific). You can also add to this thoughts on how to improve your skills further, e.g., "On my next project, I'll better research and qualify my prospects to ensure a good match and land the account."

You're Not Alone . . .

And if you are, find a way not to be. When you utilize your professional relationships to provide you with support, encouragement, opportunities, and growth, you'll soar ahead in your career. If you have good professional networks, continue to nurture and develop them. If you don't, create a plan for how to cultivate them. Don't depend on them, but rely on them for support. Always look for ways to help others in their careers; it will come back to you.

A Clear Vision

Most people know that one of the factors that makes a CEO highly effective is having a strong vision for his or her company and career. This strong vision is what makes CEOs able to motivate and positively influence others. With a great vision, people want to hear what you have to say and your message is communicated in a powerful and inspirational manner. As Jack Welch, former chairman of General Electric, has said, "Good business leaders create a vision, articulate the vision, passionately own the vision, and relentlessly drive it to completion."

When you have a vision for your career, it motivates you and decision making becomes much easier. You know what direction to take with everyday decisions because you know the direction you want to take in your career. A vision will also help you keep the bigger picture in mind and not worry about inconsequential things.

Your vision is shaped by your sense of purpose. To create a vision, you need to be aware of your core career values. You can then use these values to shape images of both what you want to ultimately achieve in your career and where you want to be now. Knowing your core values will help you decide whether you should stay on the path you're already on or take a new path.

Try to be aware of your anxiety level while creating your vision. For example, a particular vision may sound great to you but you may find yourself shying away from it because the steps to accomplish it make you nervous. If this is the case, work to overcome the anxiety and pursue your vision.

A Career Mission

Once you have a vision for your career that's fueled by your sense of purpose, you can create a specific career *mission*, which includes the objectives or ways to measure whether you are achieving your vision. A mission usually includes more tangible details and gives you an idea about what you can do to turn your vision into reality.

coaching points

1. Make a list of your core career values and goals. These are things like independence, creativity, flexible schedule, recognition, advancement, leadership, and so on. Consider how your values influence your goals and jot down everything that comes to mind. Then rank these values. Your top three to five values are the ones that you truly need to have in your career in order to feel fulfilled.
2. Use your values to create a mission for yourself (or your business). The mission can include who you want to work with as well as specific desirable results.
3. Post your vision and mission where you'll see it regularly, maybe on your computer or in your palm pilot.

Take Some Risks

Most people who thrive in their careers demonstrate an ability to take risks. While it's a myth that entrepreneurs are incredibly risk-taking compared to the average person, they definitely do take calculated risks. All of the highly successful executives and business owners I've worked with say that there was a point in time when they had to go after something that felt risky. If you feel too comfortable and experience no anxiety at all, you may need to push yourself outside of your comfort zone in order to grow.

Look at the Cost-Benefit Analysis

Anxiety doesn't like risks. It wants you to feel that things are very predictable—that things will turn out the way anxiety says they will! However, when you avoid risks, there's a cost: you stay where you are—or you may even start sliding downhill. If you move forward at all while you avoid risks, you move at a snail's pace.

Taking calculated risks (I'm not talking about going to Las Vegas and blowing all your money on slots) gives you three wonderful results: First, when you take risks, you send the message to your anxiety that you are in control; the anxiety subsides. Second, you develop confidence in yourself and your abilities. Third, you may experience an incredible outcome that wouldn't have occurred had you continued being overly careful or timid.

coaching point

If you currently have an opportunity that presents some risk or discomfort, do a cost-benefit analysis of the situation; look at the pros and cons of going after it. If you don't currently have such an opportunity, think of a future career opportunity that might come up—or one that you'd like to create for yourself—and do a cost-benefit analysis on it. Consider the benefits that might result from pushing yourself outside of your comfort zone.

Prioritize the Here and Now

The last point I'd like to make is the importance of living in the here and now. The past is in the past and the future is unknown. The only things that we can truly control are our actions today. Anxiety often takes on a future orientation—you worry about what might occur. Accept that you simply do not know and cannot control everything that might happen. If you could, life would be pretty boring! What you *can* control is what you do now.

If you're experiencing a joyful moment, enjoy it. If you're experiencing a difficult moment, accept it, and think about what you can do to improve it or learn from it. Remember: you have control over what you do right now. No one can take that from you. Own it and go after your career dreams!

Resources

Books

Albers, S. 2003. *Eating Mindfully: How to End Mindless Eating and Enjoy a Balanced Relationship with Food.* Oakland, CA: New Harbinger Publications.

Antony, M., and R. McCabe. 2004. *10 Simple Solutions to Panic: How to Overcome Panic Attacks, Calm Physical Symptoms, and Reclaim Your Life.* Oakland, CA: New Harbinger Publications.

Antony, M., and R. Swinson. 2000. *The Shyness and Social Anxiety Workbook.* Oakland, CA: New Harbinger Publications.

Bourne, E. L. 2000. *The Anxiety and Phobia Workbook.* 3rd ed. Oakland, CA: New Harbinger Publications.

Bourne, E. L. 2001. *Beyond Anxiety and Phobia.* 3rd ed. Oakland, CA: New Harbinger Publications.

Foa, E., and R. Wilson. 1991. *Stop Obsessing! How to Overcome Your Obsessions and Compulsions*. New York: Bantam.

Kabat-Zinn, K. 1994. *Wherever You Go, There You Are*. New York: Hyperion.

Kase, L., D. R. Ledley, and I. B. Weiner. 2006. *Anxiety Disorders*. Wiley Concise Guides to Mental Health. New York: John Wiley & Sons.

Leiter, M. P., and C. Maslach. 2005. *Banishing Burnout: Six Strategies for Improving Your Relationship with Work*. San Francisco: Jossey-Bass.

Paterson, R. J. 2000. *The Assertiveness Workbook: How to Express Your Ideas and Stand Up for Yourself at Work and in Relationships*. Oakland, CA: New Harbinger Publications.

Ross, J. 1994. *Triumph Over Fear*. New York: Bantam.

Stein, M., and J. Walker. 2002. *Triumph Over Shyness: Conquering Shyness and Social Anxiety*. New York: McGraw-Hill.

Walters, L. 1995. *What to Say When . . . You're Dying on the Platform*. New York: McGraw-Hill.

Weil, A. 2001. *Eating Well for Optimal Health*. New York: Quill.

Wurtman, J. 1988. *Managing Your Mind and Mood Through Food*. New York: Perennial Library.

Web sites

Anxious Nine to Five Web Site

www.AnxiousNinetoFive.com

The book's Web site; you can order the book, get free articles and tips, and hear an audio message from Larina here.

Performance and Success Coaching, LLC

www.PAScoaching.com

Larina's company Web site; offers free articles, assessments, and reports on overcoming anxiety and stress and excelling in your career. You'll also find information on speaking engagements and coaching here.

The Anxiety Disorders Association of America

www.adaa.org

A great source of information which includes a directory of anxiety specialists.

The Association for Behavioral and Cognitive Therapies

www.abct.org

Search for a therapist near you with the Find a Therapist link.

The Anxiety Panic Internet Resource

www.algy.com/anxiety

Provides self-help information for those with anxiety disorders.

Psychjourney

www.psychjourney.com

Free educational materials by top experts as well as articles, personal stories, and other resources.

Women Building Business

www.womenBuildingBusiness.com

Free teleseminars and resources for women entrepreneurs to build confidence, decrease stress and anxiety, and grow socially responsible businesses.

References

Abramowitz, J. S., D. F. Tolin, and G. P. Street. 2001. Paradoxical effects of thought suppression: A meta-analysis of controlled studies. *Clinical Psychology Review* 21: 683-703.

Antony, M. 1998. *When Perfect Isn't Good Enough*. Oakland, CA: New Harbinger Publications.

Bernstein, D., T. Borkovec, and H. Hazlett-Stevens. 2000. *New Directions in Progressive Relaxation Training: A Guidebook for Helping Professionals*. Westport, CT: Praeger Publishers.

Bourne, E. B., and L. Garano. 2003. *Coping with Anxiety: 10 Simple Ways to Relieve Anxiety, Fear, and Worry*. Oakland, CA: New Harbinger Publications.

Burns, D. D. 1980. *Feeling Good: The New Mood Therapy*. New York: Quill.

Clark, D. M. 2001. A cognitive perspective on social phobia. In *International Handbook of Social Anxiety: Concepts, Research, and Interventions Related to the Self and Shyness*, edited by W. R. Crozier and L. E. Alden. New York: John Wiley & Sons.

Costello, E. J. 1982. Locus of control and depression in students and psychiatric outpatients. *Journal of Clinical Psychology* 38(2):340-343.

Foa, E. B., M. E. Franklin, K. J. Perry, and J. D. Herbert. 1996. Cognitive biases in generalized social phobia. *Journal of Abnormal Psychology* 105:433-439.

Foa, E. B., and M. J. Kozak. 1986. Emotional processing of fear: Exposure to corrective information. *Psychological Bulletin* 99(1):20-35.

Gladwell, M. 2005. *Blink*. New York: Little Brown.

Hazlett-Stevens, H. 2005. *Women Who Worry Too Much*. Oakland, CA: New Harbinger Publications.

Huppert, J. D., D. A. Roth, and E. B. Foa. 2003. Cognitive-behavioral treatments of social phobia: New advances. *Current Psychiatry Reports* 5:189-196.

Jones, D. 2003. 2003: Year of the woman among the 'Fortune' 500? *USA Today*, December 30. http://www.USAToday.com.

Jones, E. E. 1979. The rocky road from acts to dispositions. *American Psychologist* 34:107-117.

Kelley, H. H. 1973. The process of causal attribution. *American Psychologist* 28:107-128.

Kiyosaki, R. T., and S. L. Lechter. 2000. *Rich Dad, Poor Dad: What the Rich Teach Their Kids About Money—That the Poor and Middle Class Do Not!* New York: Warner Business Books.

Marotta, P. 1999. Power-coaching for executive women. *Independent Practitioner* 19, no. 3 (Summer).

Nisbett, R. E., and L. Ross. 1980. *Human Inference: Strategies and Shortcomings of Social Judgment*. Englewood Cliffs, NJ: Prentice Hall.

Paterson, R. J. 2000. *The Assertiveness Workbook: How to Express Your Ideas and Stand Up for Yourself at Work and in Relationships.* Oakland, CA: New Harbinger Publications.

Rotter, J. B. 1966. Generalized expectancies for internal versus external control of reinforcement. *Psychological Monographs* 80:1-28.

Seligman, M. 1991. *Learned Optimism*. New York: Knopf.

Snyder, M., E. D. Tank, and E. Berscheid. 1977. Social perception and interpersonal behaviour: On the self-fulfilling nature of social stereotypes. *Journal of Personality and Social Psychology* 35:656-666.

Vitale, J. 2005. *The Attractor Factor*. New York: John Wiley & Sons.

Larina Kase, Psy.D., MBA, is a psychologist and business coach specializing in the reduction of anxiety and stress in the workplace. She worked with the renowned Center for the Treatment and Study of Anxiety at the University of Pennsylvania. As a coach, she helps business owners and executives across the Unites States and Canada to overcome workplace worries and excel in their jobs. Her work is regularly featured in media like the *New York Times, Entrepreneur Magazine*, and *Inc. Magazine.* Visit Dr. Kase on the web at **www.PAScoaching.com** and get a free e-course, "7 Steps to Career Success."

Introduction writer **Martin M. Antony, Ph.D.,** is professor in the Department of Psychiatry and Behavioural Neurosciences at McMaster University and chief psychologist and director of the Anxiety Treatment and Research Centre at St. Joseph's Healthcare, both in Hamilton, ON. Visit him on the web at **www.martinantony.com.**

Foreword writer **Joe Vitale** is the author of dozens of books, including the best-selling book *The Attractor Factor,* and an internationally recognized marketing and copywriting expert. Visit him on the web at **www.mrfire.com**.

Other New Harbinger Titles

Watercooler Wisdom
Smart tips for dealing with conflict, pressure, and change in the workplace
Item 4364, $14.95

Calming Your Anxious Mind
Use mindfulness to overcome fear, worry, and panic
Item 3384, $12.95

The Anxiety and Phobia Workbook, Fourth Edition
The classic self-help workbook for overcoming all types of anxiety
Item 4135, $19.95

Women Who Worry Too Much
Written just for women, this book is loaded with worry-busting wisdom
Item 4127, $13.95

When Perfect Isn't Good Enough
Powerful techniques for overcoming perfectionism
Item 1241, $14.95

10 Simple Solutions to Worry
Easy tips for making worry a distant memory
Item 4658, $12.95

The Daily Relaxer
The best-of-the-best techniques for finding real relaxation and genuine calm
Item 4542, $14.95

Natural Relief for Anxiety
Drug-free, whole-body approaches for overcoming anxiety
Item 3724, $12.95

available at bookstores nationwide

To order, call toll free, **1-800-748-6873,** or visit our online bookstore at **www.newharbinger.com**. Have your Visa or Mastercard number ready.

Prices subject to change without notice.